MW00961685

CONTENTS

First, I will like to thank you for taking the first step of trusting me and deciding to purchase/read this life-transforming Book. Thanks for spending your time and resources on this material.

I can assure you of exact results if you will diligently follow the exact blueprint, I lay bare in the information manual you are currently reading. It has transformed lives, and I strongly believe it will equally transform your own life too.

All the information I presented in this Do It Yourself piece is easy to digest and practice.

PUPPY TRAINING FOR BEGINNERS

CHAPTER 1

Show Your Puppy These 5 Basic Commands
Beginning

To begin on the correct foot (and paw!) with your little guy, he'll have to recognize what you anticipate from him. This will make him have a sense of safety in his capacity to meet the objectives spread out for him going ahead.

The establishment of preparing ought to be founded on encouraging feedback. Uplifting feedback is the way toward giving a pooch (or individual!) a compensation to energize the conduct you need, such as getting a check for getting down to business. The thought isn't to fix the conduct yet to prepare it utilizing something your pooch esteems. Abstain from utilizing discipline, for example, rope revisions or shouting. Discipline can make a canine become confounded and uncertain about what is being asked of him. Remember that we can't anticipate that mutts should comprehend what they don't have the foggiest idea – simply like you wouldn't expect a 2-year-old kid to realize how to tie his shoes. Persistence will go far in helping your new little dog figure out how to carry on.

Support can be anything your pooch likes. A great many people utilize little bits of a "high worth" nourishment for preparing treats — something extraordinary —, for example, dried liver or even only their kibble. Shower acclaim or the opportunity to play with a most loved toy can likewise be utilized as a prize. Mutts must be instructed to like acclaim. In the event that you give the canine a treat while saying "Great pooch!" in an upbeat voice, he will discover that acclaim is something to be thankful for and can be a prize. A few mutts like-wise appreciate petting. Nourishment is regularly the most helpful approach to fortify conduct.

Doggies can start extremely basic preparing beginning when they return home, for the most part around about two months old. Continuously continue instructional meetings brief — only 5 to 10 minutes — and consistently finish strong. On the off chance that your young doggie is experiencing difficulty learning another conduct, end the session by investigating something he definitely knows and give him a lot of recognition and a major award for his prosperity. On the off chance that your doggie gets exhausted or baffled, it will eventu-ally be counterproductive to learning.

Instruct canine to come

You'll need to start preparing a review (come when called) in a tranquil region and inside. Sit with your young doggie and state his name or "come." Each time you state "come/name," give your little dog a treat. He doesn't need to do anything yet! Simply rehash the word and give a treat. Simple!

Next, drop a treat on the floor close to you. When your little dog completes the treat on the ground, say his name once more. At the point when he looks into, give him another treat. Rehash this two or multiple times until you can start hurling the treat somewhat further away, and he can pivot to confront you when you state his name. Abstain from rehashing your pup's name; saying it time after time when he doesn't react makes it simpler for him to overlook it. Rather, draw nearer to your little dog and return to a stage where he can be fruitful at reacting to his name the first run through.

When your little dog can pivot to confront you, start including development and making the game increasingly fun! Hurl a treat on the ground and remove a couple of fast advances while calling your pup's name. They should pursue you since pursue is entertaining! At the point when they get you, give them a ton of recognition, treats or play with a pull toy. Coming to you ought to be enjoyable! Keep expanding on these games with longer separations and in different areas. When preparing outside (consistently in a sheltered, encased territory), it might be useful to keep your young doggie on a long rope from the start.

At the point when your little dog comes to you, don't connect and get him. This can be mistaking or terrifying for certain canines. In the event that your doggie is hesitant, bow and face them sideways and offer him treats as you go after the neckline. Never call your pooch to rebuff! This will just instruct him that you are eccentric, and it is a smart thought to stay away from you. Continuously reward your canine intensely for reacting to their name, regardless of whether they have been up to insidiousness!

Show a pooch to heel

In rivalry compliance preparing, "heel" signifies the canine is strolling on your left side with his head even with your knee while you hold the rope freely. Doggie preparing can be somewhat looser with the objective being that they walk cordially on a free chain without pulling. A few mentors want to state "how about we go" or "forward" rather than "heel" when they train this simple method for strolling together.

Whatever signal you pick, be reliable and consistently utilize a similar word. Regardless of whether your pup strolls on your left side or your correct side is totally up to you. In any case, be predictable about where you need them so they don't get confounded and figure out how to crisscross before you.

In the first place, ensure your young doggie is happy with wearing a chain. This can feel unusual from the outset, and a few pups may nibble the rope. Give your doggie treats as you put the chain on each time. At that point, remain beside your young doggie with the rope in a free circle and give him a few treats in succession for standing or sitting by your leg. Step advance and urge him to follow by giving another treat as he makes up for lost time.

Keep offering treats to your pup at the degree of your knee or hip as you stroll forward. At the point when he runs before you, essentially turn the other way, call him to you, and prize him set up. At that point proceed. Slowly start giving treats further separated (from each progression to each other advance, each third step, etc).

In the end your pooch will walk joyfully next to you at whatever point he's on his rope. Permit your pooch a lot of time to sniff and "enjoy the scenery" on your strolls. At the point when they've had their sniffing time, give the sign "How about we Go!" in a cheerful voice and prize them for returning into position and strolling with you.

There are two unique strategies for indicating your little dog what "sit" signifies.

The primary technique is called catching. Remain before your young doggie holding a portion of his pooch nourishment or treats. Sit tight for him to sit – state "yes" and give him a treat. At that point step in reverse or sideways to urge him to stand and hang tight for him to sit. Give another treat when they sit. After a couple of reiterations, you can start saying "sit" directly as he starts to sit.

The following alternative is called attracting. Get down before your little dog, holding a treat as a draw. Put the treat directly before the puppy's nose, at that point gradually lift the nourishment over his head. He will presumably sit as he lifts his head to snack at the treat. Enable him to eat the treat when his base contacts the ground. Rehash a couple of times with the nourishment bait, at that point expel the nourishment and utilize only your vacant hand, yet keep on compensating the young doggie after he sits. When he comprehends the hand sign to sit, you can start saying "sit" directly before you give the hand signal.

Never physically put your little dog into the sitting position; this can be befuddling or upsetting to certain mutts.

The most effective method to teach a Dog to Stay

A pup who knows the "remain" prompt will stay sitting until you request that he get up by giving another sign, called the "discharge word." Staying set up is a term conduct. The objective is to encourage your canine to stay sitting until the discharge prompt is given, at that point start including separation.

In the first place, train the discharge word. Pick which word you will utilize, for example, "alright" or "free." Stand with your young doggie in a sit or a stand, hurl a treat on the floor, and state your assertion as he ventures forward to get the treat. Rehash this a few times until you can say the word first and afterward hurl the treat AFTER he starts to move. This shows the pooch that the discharge sign intends to move your feet.

At the point when your canine realizes the discharge sign and how to sit on prompt, put him in a sit, turn and face him, and give him a treat. Delay, and give him another treat for remaining in a sit, at that point discharge him. Step by step increment the time you hold up between treats (it can sing the ABC's in your mind and stir your way up the letters in order). On the off chance that your canine gets up before the discharge sign, that is alright! It just methods he isn't prepared to sit for that long so you can make it simpler by returning to a shorter time.

When your pooch can remain in a sit for a few seconds, you can start including separation. Spot him in a sit and state "remain," make one stride back, at that point step back to the little guy, give a treat, and your discharge word. Keep working in steps, keeping it simple enough that your canine can remain effective. Practice both confronting him and leaving with your back turned (which is increasingly sensible).

When your pooch can remain, you can steadily expand the separation. This is likewise valid for the "sit." The more positively he learns it, the more he can stay sitting. The key is to not anticipate excessively, too early. Preparing objectives are accomplished in increases, so you may need to back off and center around each thing in turn. To ensure the preparation "sticks," sessions ought to be short and effective.

The most effective method to teach a Dog to Lay Down

"Down" can be instructed comparatively to "sit." You can trust that your canine will rests (starting in an exhausting, little room, for example, a washroom can help) and catch the conduct by strengthening your pooch with a treat when he rests, giving him his discharge sign to remain back up (and consolation with a draw if necessary) and afterward sitting tight for him to rests once more. At the point when he is rapidly resting subsequent to standing up, you can start saying "down" directly before he does as such.

You can likewise draw a down from a sit or remain by grasping a treat to the canine's nose and gradually carrying it to the floor. Give the treat when the pooch's elbows contact the floor to begin. After a couple of practices, start carrying your vacant hand to the floor and giving the treat AFTER he rests. At the point when he can dependably follow your hand signal, start saying "down" as you move your hand

Continue instructional courses short and fun. Finish strong. On the off chance that you feel your pooch is making some troublesome memories learning or being "difficult," assess the speed of your preparation and the estimation of your prizes. Do you have to back off and make the means simpler, or does your pooch need a greater check for a harder exercise?

The "Fundamental 5" directions will give your young doggie a solid establishment for any future preparing.

What's more, simply think, in the event that you and your young doggie keep on buckling down—and have a fabulous time—at preparing, some time or another you may become compliance champs!

Best Training Tips

Alright, he's at long last home. Preparing needs to start promptly, thinking about the new example on the carpet, also the canine's morning meal he's made of your new Manolo Blahnik strappy shoes. Be that as it may, where would it be advisable for you to begin?

Regardless of whether you train your new young doggie or canine yourself, take classes, or contract a private coach, some fundamental preparing tips ought to be handled right out of the entryway. These main 10 hints from proficient canine mentors at the highest point of their game will help make you go.

Aside: When your young doggie is mature enough, consider getting the person in question fixed or fixed, moreover on the off chance that you receive a pooch. A fixed or fixed pooch is increasingly submissive, less forceful, and might be progressively open to fruitful preparing.

Top 10 preparing tips

Pick your pooch's name carefully and be aware of it. Obviously you'll need to pick a name for your new pup or canine that you love, yet for the motivations behind preparing it likewise considers a short name finishing with a solid consonant. This enables you to state his name with the goal that he can generally hear it plainly. A solid completion (for example Jasper, Jack, Ginger) livens up young doggie ears—particularly when you place a solid stress toward the end.

On the off chance that he's a more established canine, he's most likely used to his name; in any case, transforming it isn't not feasible. On the off chance that he's from an asylum, they may disregard to reveal to you that he has a transitory name doled out to him by staff. In the event that he's from a reproducer, he'll come to you with a long name, which you might need to abbreviate, or change. Also, if he's leaving an injurious circumstance, another name may speak to a new beginning. Be that as it may, we're fortunate: hounds are very versatile. What's more, soon enough, in the event that you use it reliably, he will react to his new name.

New name or old, however much as could reasonably be expected, partner it with wonderful, fun things, as opposed to negative. The objective is for him to think about his name a similar way he considers other extraordinary stuff in his life, similar to "walk," "treat," or "supper!"

Settle on the "house rules." Before he gets back home, choose what he should or shouldn't do. Is it accurate to say that he is permitted on the bed or the furnishings? Are portions of the house beyond reach? Will he have his very own seat at your feasting table? In the event that the standards are chosen early, you can keep away from perplexity for both of you.

Set up his private cave. He needs "a room of his own." From the most punctual conceivable minute give your puppy or pooch his own, private dozing place that is not utilized by any other individual in the family, or another pet. He'll profit by brief periods took off alone in the solace and security of his lair. Prize him on the off chance that he stays loose and calm. His nook, which is frequently a case, will likewise be a significant apparatus for housetraining.

Help him loosen up when he gets back home. At the point when your pup returns home, give him a warm high temp water jug and put a ticking clock close to his resting territory. This emulates the warmth and heartbeat of his litter mates and will relieve him in his new condition. This might be considerably increasingly significant for another canine from an occupied, noisy haven who's made some harsh memories at an early stage. Whatever you can do to assist him with getting settled in his new home will be useful for both of you.

Instruct him to come when called. Come Jasper! Great kid! Encouraging him to come is the order to be aced above all else. Also, since he'll be coming to you, your alpha status will be fortified. Jump on his level and instruct him to come utilizing his name. At the point when he does, make a serious deal utilizing encouraging feedback. At that point attempt it when he's occupied with something fascinating. You'll truly observe the advantages of consummating this order right on time as he gets more established.

Prize his great conduct. Prize your pup or pooch's acceptable conduct with encouraging feedback. Use treats, toys, love, or stacks of applause. Tell him when's he's hitting the nail on the head. Similarly, never reward awful conduct; it'll just befuddle him. Deal with the bounce up. Doggies love to bounce up in welcome. Try not to criticize him, simply disregard his conduct and hold up until he settles down before giving uplifting feedback. Never empower bouncing conduct by tapping or adulating your pooch when he's in a "hopping up" position. Betray him and give him no consideration.

Show him on "hound time." Puppies and pooches live at the time. Two minutes after they've accomplished something, it's overlooked.

At the point when he's accomplishing something terrible, attempt your picked preparing system immediately so he gets an opportunity to make the relationship between the conduct and the redress. Predictable redundancy will strengthen what's he's found out.

Dishearten him from gnawing or nipping. Rather than reprimanding him, an extraordinary method to put off your bombastic canine is to imagine that you're in incredible torment when he's gnawing or nipping you. He'll be so shocked he's probably going to stop right away. In the event that this doesn't work, have a go at exchanging a bite toy for your hand or trouser leg. The swap stunt likewise works when he's into your preferred shoes. He'll incline toward a toy or bone at any rate. As a last resort, separate the gnawing conduct, and afterward simply disregard him.

Finish strong. Phenomenal kid! Great job, Jasper! He's endeavored to satisfy you all through the preparation. Leave him with loads of recognition, a treat, some petting, or five minutes of play. This ensures he'll appear at his next class with his tail swaying—prepared to work!

Canine Training for Beginners

Preparing upgrades your association with your canine and advances the bond you set up with him consistently. When you figure out how to speak with one another, you will show signs of improvement. Here are 9 essential canine preparing ventures for fledglings:

#1: Enroll in Obedience Classes

Preparing takes practice, and the additional time and exertion you put into the procedure, the more you will receive in return. In the event that this is your first canine—and regardless of whether it isn't —you might need to consider enlisting a private coach or consider pursuing an instructional course. Doggies normally begin in pup kindergarten. After that you can join an acquiescence class for more seasoned doggies. Class size for little dogs ought to be constrained to eight to ten pooch and-handler groups per teacher. This proportion empowers the teacher to give each group enough consideration and time to react to questions or extraordinary preparing conditions.

During class your little dog will become familiar with certain fundamentals, for example, sit, come, down, remain, and how to walk pleasantly on a chain. These basic exercises with an educator and different class members will show you the essentials while profiting by others' hardships.

#2: Use Positivity

Your pooch will react to your heading on the off chance that you make it fun. Creature behaviorists accept that the old methods for unforgiving rectifications may work on more than one occasion, yet they are regularly heartless and incapable over the long haul. Your pooch won't comprehend why you are furious with him.

A year-long investigation by the University of Pennsylvania, distributed in the diary Applied Animal Behavior Science (Elsevier), indicated that forceful mutts who were prepared with forceful, fierce, or aversive preparing methods, for example, being gazed at, snarled at, moved onto their backs, or hit, proceeded with their forceful ways. Non-aversive preparing techniques, for example, exercise or rewards, were extremely effective in diminishing or taking out forceful reactions.

Encouraging feedback tells your canine that you are satisfied with him, and he will rehash that conduct whenever. Prizes can comprise of nourishment, toys, or petting relying upon what your pooch reacts to best. When he gets it, reward him with nourishment, toys, or petting just a portion of the time (however verbally acclaim him unfailingly). Along these lines he'll strive to satisfy you, trusting that he'll get a prize.

#3: Keep Training Sessions Short

Start showing your pooch great habits a couple of days after he's gotten an opportunity to subside into the family unit. Keep your preparation exercises short—around 10 to 15 minutes at every session. You can rehash the session later on around the same time, however every one ought to be brief. Plan to participate in a few instructional courses a day on the grounds that no little dog figures out how to accomplish something flawlessly in just one take.

#4: Use Small Treats

It's a smart thought to give him some little treats as remunerations for preparing. You can utilize delicate business nourishment treats estimated for little dogs, bits of string cheddar, or little bits of cut-up wiener that he can swallow immediately. Keep away from hard, crunchy treats since they require a significant stretch of time to bite. Offer treats to your young doggie quickly—inside a large portion of a moment of him finishing the ideal conduct. The quicker you affirm the conduct you need, the simpler it is for your young doggie to comprehend what you're attempting to educate him. At the point when you give the prize, tail it up by saying "Great kid!"

Keep away from the snare of distributing treats during an instructional meeting on the grounds that your doggie looks charming. He will work more enthusiastically to satisfy you on the off chance that he realizes that he's getting a prize than if he hasn't earned it. On the off chance that he doesn't accomplish something you like, don't holler or rebuff. Essentially retain the prize.

#5: Say a Cue Word Only Once

State a prompt word, as "sit" or "down," just once. Mutts are savvy, so they hear your direction and can tail it the first run through. Rehashing the prompt word on different occasions doesn't enable your puppy to hone his listening abilities, and like a young person, he'll block you out.

#6: Schedule Training Before Meals

Calendar your instructional meeting before your pooch's customary dinner. Along these lines he may give nearer consideration to the guidelines with the goal that he can gain a delicious chomp.

#7: Choose a Training Time With No Distractions

Pick a period for preparing when nobody will intrude on you and you don't feel surged. Turn your mobile phone off and disregard noting the doorbell on the off chance that it rings. This will give you quality time to commit to the preparation procedure.

For the initial not many sessions, pick a room in the house that is sufficiently enormous to move around. At the point when your canine makes sense of what you need him to do, take your preparation exercises outside, ideally to a fenced-in zone, or keep him on a chain when you are in an unfenced zone. Interruptions will compete for your young doggie's consideration, so you'll have to turn out to be more fascinating than the road clamor, a quick moving squirrel, or the aroma of recently cut grass.

#8: Don't Train When Puppy's Not in the Mood

Try not to prepare your young doggie when he's hot, tired, or in lively recess. You need him engaged and enthusiastic for an instructional meeting.

#9: Don't Get Angry With Your Puppy

On the off chance that you at any point become disappointed with preparing your young doggie, don't blow up with him. Just discreetly end the session and attempt again later in the day. Numerous canines become apprehensive and will quit focusing on their mentors in the event that they are shouted at. They can get terrified of preparing and conclude that following headings isn't for them. Remain without a care in the world so your doggie will learn in a positive domain.

Instructions to Train Your Dog

Is it true that you are prepared to begin preparing your pooch or young doggie? Legitimate preparing and socialization are among your pooch's essential needs. It's imperative to begin preparing your pooch at the earliest opportunity.

From the start, hound preparing can appear to be entirely overpowering, particularly if this is your first pooch. In all actuality preparing your canine is an extremely large task. On the off chance that you make it stride by step, you will see the assignment as far less overwhelming. Here is some data to help kick you off:

Start a Dog Obedience Program: Learn how to set a fundamental establishment before you start to prepare your canine. Train Your Dog Using Games: Training your canine ought to be enjoyable! Everybody knows it's simpler to realize when you are making some acceptable memories, so take a stab at actualizing a few games into your pooch preparing routine.

Six Weeks to a Well-Trained Dog: Using this timetable as a guide, you can show your canine the essentials in around about a month and a half. Uplifting feedback: There are a wide range of approaches to prepare a canine, however most pooch experts concur that the positive way is the best for both the pooch and coach.

Need assistance with hound preparing? Consider finding support from a canine coach. Attempt bunch classes as well as private exercises, and check here for tips on reasonable pooch preparing.

House Training and Crate Training

Except if you intend to keep your pooch outside - and not many of us do in light of the fact that it's not prescribed - you'll have to show your canine where to take out. In this way, house preparing (likewise called housebreaking or potty preparing) is one of the main things you have to take a shot at with your canine. Case preparing can be an exceptionally supportive piece of the preparation procedure. This incorporates house preparing just as numerous different regions of preparing:

Container Training Dogs and Puppies: Here are the fundamentals of preparing your pooch or pup to acknowledge and even appreciate the case. Not exclusively will it help with housebreaking, yet it will likewise give your pooch his very own position.

The most effective method to House Train your Dog: When it comes down to it, house preparing isn't that confounded, however this doesn't mean it's simple. Consistency and tirelessness are key during the housebreaking procedure.

Compliant/Excitement Urination in Dogs: If your canine is as yet having mishaps in the house, it might be in excess of a basic house-breaking issue. Your pooch may pee out of fervor or to express compliant conduct.

Chain Training Dogs and Puppies

Each pooch needs to figure out how to stroll on a chain. Other than the way that most regions have chain laws, there will be times when keeping your canine on a rope is for his own security. Figure out how to acquaint your canine or little dog with the chain, at that point show him how to walk appropriately on the rope, even close to you on a bicycle. A free rope walk shows your pooch not to pull or jump when on the rope, making the experience increasingly pleasant for both you and your canine.

Step by step instructions to Socialize Dogs and Puppies

Socialization implies preparing your young doggie or grown-up pooch to acknowledge new individuals, creatures, and different places by presenting him to these things. Mingled hounds are more averse to create conduct issues and are commonly more invited by others.

Socialization can likewise help forestall the improvement of fears and fears.

Most importantly mingling your canine or young doggie will make him a more joyful, all the more polite pooch.

Clicker Training for Dogs

Clicker preparing, a typical type of encouraging feedback, is a straightforward and powerful canine preparing technique. In spite of the fact that it is still fine to prepare your canine without clicker preparing, numerous individuals think that its accommodating. With clicker preparing, you can without much of a stretch and viably show your pooch a wide range of essential and propelled directions and stunts. It's quick and simple to figure out how to clicker train your canine

Fundamental Commands and Fun Tricks

There are some fundamental canine preparing directions and pooch deceives that each canine should know like come, talk, drop it, remain, back up, and so forth. Essential directions give your pooch structure. Also, they can assist you with defeating basic pooch conduct issues and will help guard your canine.

What's better time than flaunting your canine's cool stunts?! Pooch stunts are an extraordinary method to take your canine preparing to the following level and give your pooch some psychological incitement.

Sealing Behaviors and Troubleshooting

Sealing is the last advance in preparing your canine to do any new conduct. Figure out how to verification practices so your pooch will be as respectful at the recreation center or a companion's home is he is in your very own lounge.

Keep in mind, since you have arrived at the last phases of preparing, it doesn't imply that conduct issues won't manifest. Find out about the most widely recognized pooch conduct issues and how to manage them. These aides will assist you with exploring this piece of the preparation procedure:

Sealing Behaviors: Practice practices in an assortment of circumstances with various degrees of interruption. Without sealing, your pooch may act well in your parlor, yet appear to overlook all his preparation when he is outside the house.

Show Your Dog Self-Control: This technique shows your pooch that nothing in life is free, however that he needs to gain things like nourishment and consideration through compliance.

Normal Dog Behavior Problems: Understanding potential conduct issues can assist you with recognizing and address them before things gain out of power.

Canine Behavior Management Versus Dog Training: While hound conduct the board and pooch preparing are two unique things, they are not fundamentally unrelated. Conduct the executives is a significant piece of any pooch preparing program.

Propelled Dog Training

When your canine has aced every one of the essentials, you can think about proceeding onward to further developed stunts. These exercises will help keep your pooch dynamic, fit and intellectually animated. In addition, they will help fortify the bond you share with your canine buddy.

Recall that preparation is a continuous procedure. You will never be totally wrapped up. It is critical to continue dealing with compliance preparing for the duration of the life of your pooch. Individuals who become familiar with a language at a youthful age yet quit communicating in that language may overlook a lot of it as they become more seasoned. The equivalent goes for your canine: use it or lose it. Going through even the most essential deceives and directions will assist them with remaining crisp in your canine's psyche. In addition, it's an extraordinary method to invest energy with your canine.

Instructions to Train Your Dog

Is it true that you are prepared to begin preparing your pooch or pup? Appropriate preparing and socialization are among your canine's essential needs. It's imperative to begin preparing your canine as quickly as time permits.

. . .

From the start, hound preparing can appear to be entirely overpowering, particularly if this is your first pooch. In all actuality preparing your pooch is an extremely huge task. In the event that you make it stride by step, you will see the undertaking as far less overwhelming. Here is some data to help kick you off:

Start a Dog Obedience Program: Learn how to set an essential establishment before you start to prepare your canine.

Train Your Dog Using Games: Training your pooch ought to be enjoyable! Everybody knows it's simpler to realize when you are making some acceptable memories, so take a stab at executing a few games into your canine preparing routine.

Six Weeks to a Well-Trained Dog: Using this timetable as a guide, you can show your canine the fundamentals in around about a month and a half.

Uplifting feedback: There are a wide range of approaches to prepare a canine, however most pooch experts concur that the positive way is the best for both the pooch and coach. Need assistance with hound preparing? Consider finding support from a canine coach. Attempt bunch classes and additionally private exercises, and check here for tips on reasonable canine preparing.

House Training and Crate Training

Except if you intend to keep your canine outside - and not many of us do on the grounds that it's not prescribed - you'll have to show your pooch where to dispose of. Thusly, house preparing (additionally called housebreaking or potty preparing) is one of the main things you have to deal with your canine. Box preparing can be a useful piece of the preparation procedure. This incorporates house preparing just as numerous different zones of preparing:

Container Training Dogs and Puppies: Here are the essentials of preparing your pooch or pup to acknowledge and even appreciate the carton. Not exclusively will it help with housebreaking, yet it will likewise give your canine his very own position.

Step by step instructions to House Train your Dog: When it comes down to it, house preparing isn't that muddled, yet this doesn't mean it's simple. Consistency and persistence are key during the housebreaking procedure.

Accommodating/Excitement Urination in Dogs: If your pooch is as yet having mishaps in the house, it might be in excess of a straightforward housebreaking issue. Your pooch may pee out of fervor or to express compliant conduct.

Chain Training Dogs and Puppies

Each pooch needs to figure out how to stroll on a chain. Other than the way that most territories have chain laws, there will be times when keeping your canine on a rope is for his very own wellbeing. Figure out how to acquaint your pooch or pup with the rope, at that point show him how to walk appropriately on the chain, even next to you on a bicycle. A free chain walk shows your canine not to pull or jump when on the rope, making the experience progressively charming for both you and your pooch.

Dark lab doggie on a chain, watching his proprietor

Socialization implies preparing your doggie or grown-up pooch to acknowledge new individuals, creatures, and different places by presenting him to these things. Mingled hounds are less inclined to create conduct issues and are commonly more invited by others. Socialization can likewise help forestall the advancement of fears and fears.

Basically mingling your pooch or doggie will make him a more joyful, all the more polite canine.

Clicker Training for Dogs

Clicker preparing, a typical type of encouraging feedback, is a basic and compelling pooch preparing strategy. Despite the fact that it is still fine to prepare your canine without clicker preparing, numerous individuals think that its supportive. With clicker preparing, you can without much of a stretch and viably show your canine a wide range of fundamental and propelled directions and stunts. It's quick and simple to figure out how to clicker train your canine

Fundamental Commands and Fun Tricks

There are some fundamental canine preparing directions and pooch deceives that each pooch should know like come, talk, drop it, remain, back up, and so forth. Fundamental directions give your pooch structure. Furthermore, they can assist you with beating regular canine conduct issues and will help protect your pooch.

Step by step instructions to Train Your Dog to Stay

What's better time than flaunting your canine's cool stunts?! Pooch stunts are an extraordinary method to take your canine preparing to the following level and give your pooch some psychological incitement.

Sealing Behaviors and Troubleshooting

Sealing is the last advance in preparing your canine to do any new conduct. Figure out how to verification practices so your pooch will be as loyal at the recreation center or a companion's home is he is in your own lounge.

Keep in mind, since you have arrived at the last phases of preparing, it doesn't imply that conduct issues won't manifest. Find out about the most widely recognized pooch conduct issues and how to manage them. These aides will assist you with exploring this piece of the preparation procedure:

Sealing Behaviors: Practice practices in an assortment of circumstances with various degrees of interruption. Without sealing, your canine may carry on well in your lounge, however appear to overlook all his preparation when he is outside the house.

Show Your Dog Self-Control: This technique shows your pooch that nothing in life is free, however that he needs to procure things like nourishment and consideration through dutifulness.

Regular Dog Behavior Problems: Understanding potential conduct issues can assist you with identifying and address them before things gain out of power.

Canine Behavior Management Versus Dog Training: While hound conduct the executives and pooch preparing are two unique things, they are not totally unrelated. Conduct the executives is a significant piece of any pooch preparing program.

Propelled Dog Training

When your canine has aced every one of the nuts and bolts, you can think about proceeding onward to further developed stunts. These exercises will help keep your pooch dynamic, fit and intellectually invigorated. Furthermore, they will help fortify the bond you share with your canine friend.

Recall that preparation is a continuous procedure. You will never be totally wrapped up. It is critical to continue dealing with submission preparing for the duration of the life of your canine. Individuals who get familiar with a language at a youthful age yet quit communicating in that language may overlook a lot of it as they become more established. The equivalent goes for your pooch: use it or lose it. Going through even the most essential deceives and directions will assist them with remaining crisp in your canine's psyche. Besides, it's an extraordinary method to invest energy with your pooch.

7 Most Popular Dog Training Methods

There are such huge numbers of well known canine preparing techniques out there that it tends to be baffling to discover which will be which and what strategy will be best for both your pooch and you as a proprietor.

On the off chance that you think that its staggering and confounding, you're not the only one. There is even a lot of difference inside the expert pooch preparing network about which strategies are successful and moral, and a few techniques cover or are utilized couple for the best outcomes.

1. Encouraging feedback

Absolutely uplifting feedback is a strategy advanced via mentors like Dawn Sylvia-Stasiewicz, who prepared the Obamas' pooch, Bo. The hypothesis behind it is genuinely direct. Mutts will rehash great conduct when it's trailed by a prize. Awful conduct doesn't get a prize or affirmation. In the event that amendment needs to occur, it comes as evacuation of remunerations, similar to a toy or treat being removed. Cruel censures or physical disciplines aren't fundamental. This preparation technique starts with compensating an ideal conduct promptly, inside seconds after it occurs. That way the canine comes to connect the conduct with the prize.

A few mentors join this strategy with clicker preparing (see number three beneath). This offers the pooch an unmistakable hint of the precise minute the conduct was finished. Directions likewise should be short and to the point. Sit. Remain. Come.

Uplifting feedback requires consistency. In this manner, everybody in your family unit needs to utilize similar directions and prize framework.

Start with ceaseless rewards each time your pooch makes the best decision. At that point, slowly move to discontinuous prizes as the conduct gets reliable. At times apprentice coaches inadvertently reward terrible conduct. For instance they may let the canine outside when they start yelping at a squirrel or another pooch. Just needed practices get rewards, which can incorporate treats, toys, acclaim, and pets? It can likewise be anything but difficult to overload when your pooch is adapting, so utilize little treats when you are remunerating with nourishment.

This technique is extraordinary for learning directions, however you need tolerance for adjusting undesirable practices.

2. Logical Training

Science-based canine preparing can be hard to characterize as it depends on data that is ceaselessly assembling and evolving. It expects to comprehend mutts' tendency, their capacity to be adapted, and the viability of remunerations and disciplines.

Creature behaviorists are continually making new investigations and tests to shape our comprehension of canine brain science. Mentors depend on these investigations to work with hounds. Before a conduct is adjusted, everything about that conduct must be comprehended.

Since science-based canine preparing is so expansive, it's difficult to pinpoint a general procedure behind it. Truth be told, a ton of the strategies utilized in logical pooch preparing are utilized by different types of preparing. Generally, there is a dependence on operant molding, which for the most part incorporates uplifting feedback and, less regularly, a few types of discipline.

· · ·

Some logical mentors accept that it's additionally essential to figure out how to reinforce great conduct without the requirement for remunerations and to depend on hound brain research to discover approaches to improve off-rope connections among proprietors and their puppies.

Logical preparing depends on doing a decent arrangement of research and staying refreshed on the most recent examinations. Therefore, it might be best for proficient coaches, since the strategies they utilize are regularly powerful whether you know the science behind them or not, and different types of preparing as of now utilize a considerable lot of those techniques.

Additionally, growing new strategies dependent on research may not be fitting for everybody. All things considered, it's a smart thought for hound proprietors to remain educated and focus on new research when it gets accessible.

3. Clicker Training

Clicker preparing is likewise founded on operant molding and depends vigorously on indistinguishable standards from uplifting feedback. Actually, clicker preparing might be gathered in as a technique for encouraging feedback, as opposed to as its own type of preparing.

It depends on the utilization of a gadget to make a snappy, sharp commotion, for example, a whistle or, as the name recommends, a clicker to motion toward a canine when a needed conduct is practiced.

The benefit of utilizing clicker preparing is that it flags the careful minute the ideal conduct is done and precisely what is being remunerated. Mentors would then be able to utilize the clicker to shape new practices and include verbal directions. Initially, the canine should be adapted to realize that a tick implies a prize is coming. At that point the pooch can connect a conduct with a tick and a prize. At long last, the verbal order can be acquainted with structure another affiliation.

This is an extraordinary strategy for adapting new deceives, and it can help shape the nuts and bolts into increasingly convoluted errands. Numerous expert coaches utilize this technique.

While it is incredible for adapting new practices, clicker preparing isn't really appropriate for checking undesirable practices. At the point when utilized close by other preparing strategies, it tends to be successful in ensuring you have a well-prepared, polite pooch.

4. Electronic Training

A youthful Boston terrier hound watching eagerly just wondering. Electronic preparing depends on the utilization of an electric neckline that conveys a stun or a shower of citronella when a pooch isn't playing out an ideal assignment. It's generally utilized for preparing a good ways off when a chain can't be utilized.

For instance, stun collars can prepare a canine to remain inside limits of an un-fenced yard. Remote collars can instruct pooches to work in fields or do chasing work. Individuals who utilize these gadgets guarantee that there's less danger of a pooch getting injured than with stifle collars or other mechanical gadgets. There are numerous issues with this preparation technique. One is that it depends on discipline for awful conduct rather than remunerations, which means a canine realizes what they shouldn't do, as opposed to what they ought to do.

Another issue is that it can make a lot of pressure and lead to changeless uneasiness issues for hounds. The gadgets are regularly utilized by unpracticed proprietors, and accordingly are abused. This can cause a great deal of superfluous torment, both physically and mentally, for hounds.

Proficient canine mentors may see wanted outcomes from electronic preparing, however it's certainly not for use by normal proprietors. There are numerous options that put mutts under far less pressure and torment. In case you're going to utilize an electronic gadget, counsel an expert about appropriate utilize and think about an elective type of conduct redress.

5. Model-Rival Or Mirror Training

The model-rival technique for preparing depends on the way that canines learn by perception. By giving a model of good conduct or an opponent to seek assets, hounds figure out how to mirror practices.

So a mentor may have another human go about as the model, applauding them for finishing undertakings on direction or chiding them for undesirable conduct. The canine, as a spectator, gains what to do effectively from the model.

The model can likewise go about as an opponent, contending to do the correct errand for an ideal toy or treat as a prize, urging the canine to get on the undertaking and achieve it all the more rapidly. Mirror preparing depends on a similar rule, utilizing the pooch proprietor as a model, at that point offering awards for imitating great conduct. It utilizes the pooch's common senses to work socially as opposed to neutralizing them. Basically, the pooch learns by model. This preparation strategy works with a comparable degree of achievement as encouraging feedback and operant molding. Be that as it may, a few coaches may think that it's increasingly common and ideal.

In the event that your canine has a solid bond with you and can invest a great deal of energy watching you and chasing after you, this might be a strategy that you discover more agreeable than adhering to ordinary instructional courses.

6. Alpha Dog Or Dominance

Back perspective on a man strolling a gathering of mutts

Alpha pooch or predominance preparing depends on a canine's instinctual pack mindset to make a relationship of accommodation and strength.

The hypothesis recommends that mutts consider their to be as their packs and follow a social pecking order, as saw in hostage wolf packs. At the point when a pooch considers themselves to be the alpha, they have to figure out how to rather regard their human as the alpha and submit.

A few strategies utilized in this procedure incorporate understanding pooch non-verbal communication and reacting in like manner, anticipating certainty and authority, and going first with regards to eating, going into or leaving rooms, or strolling on rope.

In the event that your pooch needs to go out, at that point they need to sit before you open the entryway. On the off chance that they need to eat, at that point they need to stand by smoothly while you get ready nourishment.

For the most part with alpha preparing, you don't permit your pooch on furniture with you, including the bed. You likewise don't get down to your canine's eye level. That is on the grounds that these are signs that your pooch has equivalent remaining in the relationship. You are in control; you are predominant.

Cesar Millan promoted this preparation strategy. In any case, he here and there consolidates strength preparing with different strategies when proper.

Some advanced coaches state this procedure is obsolete, as new research has indicated that mutts don't depend on pack mindset as much as recently suspected, and the pack dynamic of wolves isn't organized in the wild a similar way it was the point at which the creatures were seen in captivity.

TECHNIQUES TO TRAIN YOUR PUPPY AND POTTY TRAINING

CHAPTER 2

The most effective method to Potty Train a Puppy: A Comprehensive Guide for Success

Cases are a significant young doggie housetraining device that can make your life simpler.

Young dogie cushions and paper preparing offer a brief answer for housetraining. Consistency, consideration, comprehension, and persistence are generally key in house training. Potty preparing your doggie is one of the first and most significant stages a canine proprietor can take to get ready for a cheerful, solid concurrence with their pets. It's critical to do examine ahead of time, and make a point to detail an arrangement and calendar dependent on how much time you can give to your canine's house training.

Case preparing is a fundamental piece of potty preparing achievement. As cave creatures, pooches can acknowledge cases as a sheltered space, and as spotless animals, they'll frequently need to keep that rest space clean. A container of the correct size is significant, as one that is too enormous may persuade the puppy they have space to both rest and dispense with. Little dog cushions give hounds the choice of mitigating themselves in an affirmed spot inside. Nonetheless, these can be precarious to prepare with in case you're extreme objective is to get the puppy to just potty outside in the end.

While housetraining, perception and supervision are significant, as is keeping to a timetable to make things simpler on your pooch. Contingent upon the canine, potty preparing can take up to months, so tolerance is vital, as is consistency all through preparing.

House Training Your Puppy

When to Begin House Training Puppy Steps for Housetraining Your Puppy Using a Crate to House Train Puppy Signs That Your Puppy Needs to Eliminate House Training Setbacks Do's and Don'ts in Potty Training Your Puppy

House preparing your little dog is about consistency, persistence, and uplifting feedback. The objective is to impart acceptable propensities and fabricate a caring bond with your pet. It normally takes 4-6 months for a pup to be completely house prepared, however a few little dogs may take as long as a year. Size can be an indicator. For example, littler breeds have littler bladders and better capacities to burn calories and require progressively visit trips outside. Your doggy's past living conditions are another indicator. You may find that you have to enable your pup to bring an end to old propensities so as to build up progressively alluring ones.

And keeping in mind that you're preparing, don't stress if there are misfortunes. For whatever length of time that you proceed with an administration program that incorporates taking little dog out at the main sign he needs to go and offering him rewards, he'll learn.

When to Begin House Training Puppy

Specialists suggest that you start house preparing your doggy when he is between 12 weeks and four months old. By then, he has enough control of his bladder and defecations to figure out how to hold it.

In the event that your doggy is more established than 12 weeks when you bring him home and he's been killing in an enclosure (and perhaps eating his waste), house preparing may take longer. You should reshape the canine's conduct - with consolation and prize.

Steps for Housetraining Your Puppy

Specialists prescribe keeping the pup to a characterized space, regardless of whether that implies in a box, in a room, or on a chain. As your little dog discovers that he needs to go outside to do his business, you can step by step give him more opportunity to meander about the house.

At the point when you begin to house train, follow these means:

Keep the pup on a normal encouraging calendar and remove his nourishment between dinners.

Take pup out to take out before anything else and afterward once like clockwork to 60 minutes. Likewise, consistently take him outside after dinners or when he wakes from a snooze. Ensure he goes out last thing around evening time and before he's disregarded.

Take little dog to a similar recognize each opportunity to do his business. His fragrance will incite him to go. Remain with him outside, at any rate until he's home prepared.

At the point when your little dog kills outside, acclaim him or give him a treat. A stroll around the area is a decent prize.

Step by step instructions to Potty Train a Puppy: Tips for New Pet Parents

When concluding how to potty train a little dog, or a recently embraced canine, you have two alternatives—train them to mitigate themselves outside, or inside your home on a pee cushion and afterward change them to the outside. We'll take you through the two choices and give you tips to join box potty preparing into your arrangement.

The most effective method to Train a Puppy to Pee Outside

Your pup can't disclose to you they need to diminish themselves, or can they? They can in the event that you show them a "potty prompt." Potty signs start by telling your pet the best way to flag they need to go outside. From that point, your little dog will connect the sentiment of peeing with being outside of your home. Here's the manner by which to begin:

Stage 1: Teach your little dog the potty prompt

Have your little dog sit by the indirect access. At the point when your pet barks, open the indirect access and let them out. Or maybe not show your little guy to bark? Attempt a ringer. At the point when your pet rings the chime, open the entryway and take them outside. Keep in mind, the potty sign is only for going potty, don't let your little dog play a lot outside in the wake of doing their business - else, they will connect the prompt with getting the opportunity to play outside, not simply going potty.

What to do on the off chance that you have to change the potty sign

So you instructed your pup to bark when they have to go to the restroom, yet now they bark constant. You can have a go at showing them another signal like sitting at the entryway. You could even place a floor covering by the entryway, and train your doggy to realize that when they sit on the mat, you open the entryway. From here, rehash stages two and three to finish your pet's retraining.

Stage 2: Determine a set potty territory

Put your little dog on a chain and walk them out to the piece of the yard you need your pooch to mitigate themselves at. Try not to keep strolling. Rather, trust that your pet will soothe themselves. At the point when your little dog does, reward them with treats and verbal applause. This will make peeing outside a positive encounter. On the off chance that they don't go, take your little dog back in the house and rehash. They will get on quick.

Stage 3: Use a box when you're not home

28

At the point when you aren't home with your pet, keep them to a territory, for example, a box. This helps limit mishaps in your room, family room, or whatever other zones when you aren't there to hear or see the prompt.

The Indoors-to-Outdoors Method

On the off chance that you don't have a yard, or your doggy is finishing their shots, it might be ideal to start potty preparing inside and afterward progress your pet to the outside. To start preparing your canine to mitigate themselves in the right spot inside, you'll have to figure out how to potty train a little dog on cushions, or how to begin with case potty preparing.

Step by step instructions to potty train a little dog on cushions

Decide a kept territory to start house preparing—like the washroom or the pantry (preferably some place with simple to clean floors if there should arise an occurrence of mishaps!). Whichever zone you choose, ensure it's pup sealed and evacuate any hurtful items. Next, set up the space by covering the floor with pee cushions and putting your pet's bed in an edge of the room.

To assist you with beginning with a daily schedule, here are a few stages you can follow:

- Stage 1: Change pee cushions frequently however place a little bit of the dirty cushion over the perfect cushion in the zone you need your pup to pee. The aroma reminds your pup that this region is the restroom.
- Stage 2: Remove the pee cushions nearest to your pet's bed once your little dog is peeing in a similar zone.
- Stage 3: Continue evacuating the pee cushions until you have expelled everything except a couple of sheets.

At the point when you have reliable accomplishment with your pup just utilizing a couple of pee cushions, you can steadily grow the region they approach. In the event that mishaps start to happen, diminish the zone. For pet guardians who intend to progress their little dog to an indoor or yard grass "potty," move the papers close to this spot. Presently, you're prepared to show your little dog a potty prompt so they can assuage themselves outside.

Carton potty preparing

Before you start carton potty preparing, you need the correct size control. Remember your pet just needs enough space to stand up, pivot, and rests. Any more space will urge them to diminish themselves in one corner and rest in another. A few cases accompany dividers so you can change the size as they develop.

To get your pup used to their carton, hurl a treat in and enable them to head inside and return out. Acclaim your little dog each time they enter. Stir your way up to your pet going through 10 minutes in their carton and afterward longer once they're agreeable. At the point when your little dog relates their box as their living space, container potty preparing starts. Rather than ruining the zone where they rest and eat, they'll let you realize they have to go. Like other potty preparing techniques, building up a routine is vital. Inside fifteen minutes of eating, drinking or playing, your pup ought to have the chance to calm themselves. For more tips on box potty preparing, look at our carton preparing guide.

To what extent Does it Take to Potty Train a Puppy?

There is no characterized time span with regards to how to potty train a doggy. There are numerous components that become possibly the most important factor, with consistency being the most significant. Make certain to compensate your little dog when they follow their preparation plan.

Managing mishaps

Mishaps will happen regardless of the amount you attempt to forestall them. It's a matter of deciding the reason and strengthening positive conduct. Perceiving when your pet is pushed or what ceaselessly triggers mishaps will assist you with concocting restorative measures. For tidying up messes, make certain to give the grimy zone a decent cleaning. Pet-safe stain removers and scent removers are acceptable cleaning items to have close by.

Remember that even a house prepared little dog will have mishaps when all over the place. To restrict this conduct, keep your little dog's timetable as reliable as could be expected under the circumstances. In case you're going out traveling or visiting companions, take your little dog on a long stroll with loads of chances to discharge their bladder in advance. Bringing toys is another valuable strategy, as they can help keep your pet concentrated on an action.

Potty preparing a pup requires some serious energy and duty, so don't become irritated. At the point when you feel your pet is straying off base, come back to the essentials. Whichever strategy you pick, stick to it and build up a daily practice. With uplifting feedback, your pet will start to perceive when they are indicating acceptable conduct. Remain arranged by shopping all the potty preparing supplies you'll require!

House-preparing your pooch or little dog requires tolerance, responsibility and heaps of consistency. Mishaps are a piece of the procedure, yet in the event that you follow these fundamental house-preparing rules, you can get the most up to date individual from your family progressing nicely in half a month's time.

Build up a daily schedule

Like children, young doggies do best on a customary timetable. The calendar instructs them that there are times to eat, times to play and times to do their business. As a rule, a doggy can control their bladder one hour for each period of age. So if your little dog is two months old, they can hold it for around two hours. Try not to go longer than this between restroom breaks or they're ensured to have a mishap.

Take your doggy outside regularly—somewhere around like clock-work—and following they wake up, during and subsequent to playing, and in the wake of eating or drinking.

Pick a restroom spot outside, and consistently take your little dog (on a rope) to that spot. While your pup is assuaging themselves, utilize a particular word or expression that you can in the long run use before they go to remind them what to do. Take them out for a more extended walk or some recess simply after they have wiped out.

Prize your little dog each time they dispose of outside. Acclaim or give treats—yet make sure to do so following they've completed, not after they return inside. This progression is crucial, on the grounds that remunerating your pooch for going outside is the best way to train what's anticipated from them. Prior to fulfilling, be certain they're done. Doggies are effectively diverted and in the event that you acclaim too early, they may neglect to complete until they're back in the house. Put your little dog on a customary bolstering plan. What goes into a doggy on a calendar leaves a pup on a timetable. Contingent upon their age, young doggies for the most part should be bolstered three or four times each day. Sustaining your pup at similar occasions every day will make it almost certain that they'll dispose of at steady occasions too, making housetraining simpler for both of you.

Get your little dog's water dish around over two hours before sleep time to lessen the probability that they'll have to ease themselves during the night. Most young doggies can rest for roughly seven hours without requiring a restroom break. In the event that your little dog wakes you up in the night, don't overemphasize it; else they will think the time has come to play and won't have any desire to return to rest. Turn on as barely any lights as could reasonably be expected, don't converse with or play with your doggy, take them out and afterward return them to bed.

Administer your pup

Try not to offer your pup a chance to soil in the house; watch out for them at whatever point they're inside.

Tie your pup to you or a close by household item with a six-foot chain in the event that you are not effectively preparing or playing. Watch for signs that your pup needs to go out. A few signs are self-evident, for example, yelping or scratching at the entryway, hunching down, fretfulness, sniffing around or orbiting. At the point when you see these signs, promptly snatch the rope and take them outside to their washroom spot. On the off chance that they take out, acclaim them and award with a treat.

Keep your little dog on chain in the yard. During the house-training procedure, your yard ought to be dealt with like some other room in your home. Give your pup some opportunity in the house and yard simply after they become dependably housetrained.

At the point when you can't manage, restrict

At the point when you can't watch your little dog consistently, limit them to a territory little enough that they won't have any desire to take out there.

Peruse Dog Crates on Amazon.com

The space ought to be sufficiently huge to serenely stand, rests and pivot. You can utilize a part of a restroom or pantry closed off with child entryways. Or then again you might need to container train your doggy. (Make certain to figure out how to utilize a box others consciously as a strategy for repression.) If your doggy has gone through a few hours in control, you'll have to take them straightforwardly to their washroom spot when you return.

Mix-ups occur

Anticipate that your pup should have a couple of mishaps in the house—it's an ordinary piece of housetraining. This is what to do when that occurs:

Interfere with your doggy when you get them in the demonstration.

Cause a frightening clamor (to be mindful so as not to terrify them) or state "OUTSIDE!" and promptly take them to their washroom spot. Applause your little guy and give a treat on the off chance that they finish there. Try not to rebuff your little dog for taking out in the house. On the off chance that you locate a grimy zone, it's past the point where it is possible to direct a redress. Simply tidy it up. Shaming puppy with it, taking them to the spot and reprimanding them or some other discipline will just make them terrified of you or reluctant to dispose of in your essence. Discipline will regularly accomplish more damage than anything else. Clean the filthy zone completely. Little dogs are profoundly energetic to keep dirtying in regions that smell like pee or defecation.

Doggy potty preparing is one of the principal things you'll do to assist you with hounding get to know his new home, and there are numerous approaches. Attempt these seven proposals to set you and your canine up for progress.

1. Adhere to a Potty Spot

Before you start little dog potty preparing your new buddy, choose where you'd like him to "go" outside of the house. Do you have a yard? Direct him to an area that is snappy to get to from the entryway. Loft abiding mutts ought to likewise have the option to recognize common, simple to-arrive at ground that isn't impeding pedestrian activity—or autos, so far as that is concerned.

When you've figured out where you'll bring your pooch during this preparation stage, ensure you take him to a similar region each time he goes outside to do his business. Mutts can smell their domain, so consistency is significant when you're house preparing a little dog.

2. Get familiar with the Signs of Needing to Go

Your new little dog probably won't communicate in a similar language, yet he's attempting to reveal to you that he needs to dispose of. Fortunately there are sure signs for which you can watch out. Quickly bring your canine outside to his extraordinary potty spot when you see him:

West Highland White Terrier holding up at the front entryway of a home

- Smelling his back
- Pacing around and around
- Yapping or scratching at the entryway
- Sniffing the floor
- Hunching down.

He may give the last indication a piece past the point of no return, yet be prepared to open the entryway at any rate so he will realize that his typical zone is available to all before he goes in an inappropriate spot.

You'll have to rapidly bring your canine outside when you see any of these signs, so prepare. Keep a chain directly at the entryway, enabling you to usher him outside as fast as could be expected under the circumstances. Furthermore, when he realizes where his uncommon potty region is, he'll profit to it just for his own. Simply remember to pick a similar detect each time your pooch needs to ease himself.

3. Make Meal Time the Same Time

At the point when house preparing a pup, keep all supper and bite times planned. This is useful for two reasons: First, planned dinners will train your canine when he can hope to eat for the duration of the day. Second, in case you're bolstering your canine at explicit occasions, you can development and carry him to his potty spot with the desire that he'll be all set not long after he completes the process of eating.

4. The Water Bowl

On the off chance that your pooch is a substantial water-consumer, odds are he'll be a successive urinator also. To preclude any mishaps, take your doggy out soon after drinking during the little dog potty preparing stage so he's in the opportune spot at the ideal time.

5. Go Outside Often

In the event that you need to be certain your canine keeps the potty outside, you'll need to bring him out yourself routinely. When in doubt it is a smart thought to take your little guy out before anything else, after all feedings, and whenever you see any signals that he may need to go. For extremely youthful young doggies, it is regularly a smart thought to take him out each hour to maintain a strategic distance from mishaps until you show signs of improvement thought of how frequently he does his business. At that point, after some time you can stretch the time between trips outside until you're certain that he will reveal to you when he needs to go out without anyone else. You ought to likewise bring your pooch outside just before you rest—your 3 a.m. self with thank you for it. Canines ought to be brought outside inside thirty minutes of each sustaining to empower a solid discharge.

6. Applause Helps

Everybody likes to realize when they're working admirably, and your doggy will flourish with this encouraging feedback. It doesn't make a difference on the off chance that you acclaim him with treats or state "great job" while petting him. Simply put forth sure he realizes you value his attempts to do things the correct way.

7. Smoothly Address Accidents

At the point when your canine takes out in your house, be quiet and gathered when tending to the circumstance. Divert him outside into his assigned potty spot immediately, yet comprehend that mishaps are a characteristic piece of the house preparing process. Have persistence and don't surrender! Never rebuff a pooch for mishaps since it might exacerbate things and result in more mishaps in the home.

The most significant thing you can do is spotless the region as fast and as most ideal as. In the event that your pooch smells pee or excrement in your home, he'll be confounded and believe it's fine to diminish himself there later on. For whatever length of time that he realizes where to stamp his domain, he'll have less issues. When cleaning the dirty spot, try to utilize pet-safe cleaners and get him far from the region while it dries.

8. Planning for Varying Situations

There are various circumstances that may come up during your pup's potty preparing stage for which you will need to be readied. The following are a couple of situations to prepared yourself against:

Acquainting Your Puppy with New People and Places

In the wake of getting another little guy, you will probably need to show him off to loved ones. The energy of welcome any new more bizarre can in some cases be a lot for your canine's bladder to deal with. Knowing this early can assist you with planning to maintain a strategic distance from mishaps. Ensure you take him out before you acquaint him with anybody new during the potty preparing stage; this remembers both for your own home or another spot. Moreover, on the off chance that you take your puppy to a companion or relative's home with different pooches he may sniff around and attempt to check his region, so try to watch out for him and take him outside much of the time. He can check the same number of shrubs as he needs outside the home.

Going with a House Training Puppy

Because you get another doggy doesn't mean you need to put your life on hold. You may in any case be allured to take an excursion to discover better climate and energy. If so you have to choose whether or not you are going to take him with you or have somebody watch him while you're gone. On the off chance that you choose to take him with you, it is significant that you take him out before you leave and stop each couple of hours to let him do his business. Nobody in the vehicle will need to manage a vehicle that scents like canine pee the entire outing... or then again more terrible. On the off chance that you choose to board your doggy or have a relative/companion watch your pooch, make a point to tell them that he is in potty preparing. Give them bit by bit guidelines on how you've been functioning with him to keep it reliable. There are less things harder for a canine to comprehend than when there isn't consistency in his preparation.

Getting ready for Bad Weather

Without a doubt, you'll experience some awful climate eventually during your pooch's potty preparing stage, so you'll need to be set up for it. On the off chance that it is coming down, you can't anticipate that your canine should hold his bladder so make a point to hold a huge umbrella near the entryway to keep both you and your pooch dry. Additionally, having a towel to get dry his feet after you go outside will help abstain from tidying up an alternate kind of mishap of sloppy paws on everything. On the off chance that it snows, your new puppy may be somewhat befuddled on what this new white stuff is that is everywhere throughout the ground. It's alright to allow him to investigate and play in it a bit, yet remember that pooches can get cold similarly as people, so you'll need to restrict his investigating and ensure he does his business. In the event that he has a typical spot where he goes to the restroom, you might need to take a snow scoop and scoop out a way to it so he can assuage himself in a progressively natural manner. Once more, consistency is key when preparing your little guy.

Moving

Regardless of whether your pooch is another little dog or a well-prepared grown-up hound, choosing to move starting with one spot then onto the next can now and then put extra weight on your canine. Remember this as he will need to investigate your new residence, and may even attempt to stamp his domain. To assist him with adapting to his new environment, quickly take him out to the spot where you might want him to ease himself as you did at your past home. Take him out every now and again to this spot, and prize him with applause or treats when he goes to the washroom here to revamp his relationship with a decent conduct. It may likewise be a smart thought to limit him to little territories of the new home until he begins to turn out to be increasingly acquainted with his washroom schedule. You would prefer not to wind up finding an astonishment in a piece of the house in which you didn't realize he approached.

Whatever the circumstance, the best thing you can do is to attempt to keep your fuzzy closest companion quiet. Energized, focused, or terrified pooches are increasingly inclined to mishaps in the home, regardless of whether they are the best prepared canine.

9. Bigger Issues

At long last, if your preparation doesn't appear to be taking with your pooch it may merit an excursion to the veterinarian. Visit peeing or pooping in the house can be an indication of a bigger medical problem. In the event that this is something you think, contact your vet's office promptly and let them think about your anxiety. They may just prescribe a straightforward change to your preparation standard or a change to his nourishment, yet for bigger issues you'll be happy you called in the near future.

The most effective method to Potty Train A Dog

Potty preparing hounds isn't exceptionally simple, however everybody who imparts their lives to hounds must do it. Instructions to house train a doggy is somewhat not quite the same as how to house train a pooch, however the devices, schedules and human duty levels required to do it well are the equivalent. For as long as 16 years, I have been showing little dog kindergarten and pre-adult pooch classes at The Canine Connection, my instructional hub in Chico, California. The quantity of alumni of my classes is likely in excess of 1,000 little dogs – yet it feels like I've addressed customer inquiries regarding potty preparing in any event a million times. What's once again, on the off chance that it assists somebody with living all the more cheerfully and amicably with their new canine or little dog?

Potty-preparing circumstances are of three sorts: (1) hounds who have never taken in the proper spot "to go," (2) hounds who were once housetrained yet are having a preparation relapse, and (3) hounds who are pottying automatically – that is, they have no power over their pee or poop. It simply occurs with no expectation and frequently without the canine in any event, acknowledging it is occurring by any stretch of the imagination. How about we take a gander at these all together.

Housetraining For the Never-Housetrained Dog

Maybe you have a spic and span little guy or a recently received high schooler or more seasoned pooch. One thing that is essentially imperative to building a glad interspecies family unit is that your new canine becomes housetrained as fast and dependably as could reasonably be expected. You ought to be prepared and prepared to begin housetraining your new canine from the minute that you bring him home.

Housetraining includes something other than realizing where to potty; mutts and little dogs should likewise figure out how to "hold it" until they get to a proper potty area and how to tell you to get them there. To assist hounds with building these abilities and to help keep us on track with our housetraining obligations, I urge individuals to consider housetraining as far as C.R.A.P. Each letter of the abbreviation represents a significant piece of the housetraining program: Confinement, Routine, Attention, Platinum rewards.

house preparing a pooch

The most effective method to House-Train A Dog

Restriction

Keeping your pooch from pottying in an inappropriate spot is the first and most significant housetraining task. Since the majority of us can't keep our eyes on our mutts consistently, having a sheltered, agreeable restriction zone is critical to housetraining achievement. Most mutts normally abstain from going potty in their resting zones, so limiting your pooch in a little enough region that is more bed-like than room-like forestalls undesirable mishaps as well as will assist him with creating gut and bladder control.

What are suitable repression zones? I am a gigantic devotee of cases, utilized suitably, when mutts are alright with them. A territory that is fenced off with a compact exercise pen or a littler room, (for example, a restroom or pantry with an infant entryway over the entryway) can likewise fill in as a control zone.

The key is that any restriction territory ought to be little and comfortable enough for your canine that he will pick "holding it" over pottying in it. At the point when repression is set up and utilized fittingly, there will be a reduction in potty mishaps and an expansion in entrail and bladder control.

As your pooch appreciates proceeded with progress at pottying outside fittingly and not pottying inside, you can build the size of the territory where he is bound when not being regulated. Try not to go excessively far, giving him entire house opportunity after he hasn't had a mishap for a couple of days. Rather, utilize an activity pen to grow his repression territory by, state, 50 to 100 square feet more for every seven day stretch of accomplishment.

Schedule

The two canines and people profit by an anticipated, steady house-training schedule. This routine should represent imprisonment time, potty breaks, dinner times, play time, preparing time, strolls, and the various improving exercises that are a piece of your pooch's day by day life.

I suggest my customers make a composed schedule that incorpo-rates potty breaks at least consistently or two, contingent upon the age and circumstance of the canine. The general standard for "holding it" in a case or pen is that canines ought to be able to hold their guts and bladder, in hours, the quantity of months they are in addition to one. In this way, a three-month-old little guy should have the option to hold his pee and crap for four hours. In any case, there are such huge numbers of special cases to this standard; most quite, that move-ment frequently causes a puppy to need to "go." The best schedules, at that point, depend on a strong comprehension of your canine.

Some significant notes about potty breaks:

1. You should go with your canine to the potty zone so you can remunerate the deed when it happens. By conveying a prompt prize, your pooch rapidly comes to comprehend that "Goodness my gosh, going pee or crap in this area is out and out splendid!"

2. It very well may be extremely valuable to show your pooch a prompt for pottying conduct. A few people utilize the straightforward expression, "Go potty!" Others utilize a code word, for example, "Get occupied!" Whatever expression you use, say it once just before he starts to potty (don't state it again and again), and afterward prize and commendation him relentlessly when he's set. Before long, he will comprehend that the expression is a signal – a chance to gain prizes for doing what he currently realizes it implies: going potty. This will enable him to comprehend what you need when you take him to go potty in another condition, or under diverting conditions he has not yet experienced.

3. On the off chance that you anticipate that your canine should potty on-and off-rope, your potty trips with your pooch ought to now and again be on-rope and here and there off-rope. Why? From a pooch's perspective, pottying while on-versus off-chain can be an altogether different encounter. Acquainting him with both will pay off later on.

4. While it may appear to be helpful to have a pooch who will potty just in your yard (I call these private pottyers), it's significant that your canine figures out how to potty in other outside spots, as well. In fact, I need pooches to be open pottyers (with capable gate-keepers who will tidy up after them) so day and even medium-term excursions are agreeable for all. I feel sorry for the poor canine who has figured out how to potty just in the protection of his home when his family chooses to expedite him a long get-away!

5. Likewise in light of a legitimate concern for flexibility to new conditions, pooches ought to be presented to various surfaces as a component of housetraining. Canines can create "substrate inclina-tion," the ability to potty just on explicit surfaces, for example, grass or cement.

While your pooch's tendency to build up an inclination for pottying on specific substrates can be useful in making a character-ized latrine space in your yard, it can likewise restrict your canine's flexibility to new conditions on the off chance that he isn't enabled the choice to potty on various substrates.

6. Potty excursions ought to be mission-driven. on the off chance

that your pooch will in general fiddle and skip preceding pottying, limit your canine's entrance to play until the deed is finished. Fiddling and skipping would then be able to turn out to be a piece of the prize.

7. On the off chance that you are away from your home for expanded timeframes during the day, you should have an arrangement for getting your pooch to his potty spot in your nonappearance. At times it takes a town to housetrain a canine, with companions, family, and neighbors, maybe helped by proficient pet sitters, hound walkers, or mentors assisting with the potty trip shifts.

Consideration

The primary inquiry I pose to when a customer asks me an inquiry about a trouble with their pooch's housetraining is: "Are you getting your canine in the demonstration of pottying improperly or simply finding the proof sometime later?" More frequently than not, individuals timidly admit that they as a rule discover the wreckage afterward – and this consistently implies their consideration should be improved. There are two tremendous advantages to keeping up a laser center around your pooch when he isn't bound. To begin with, you can begin to perceive and compensate your canine's "gotta go" signals. At the point when your canine starts to pace, circle, and sniff, you can cheer his flagging ("Awesome doggie! How about we go, go, GO!") and surge him to his potty spot. Remunerating "gotta go" signs will urge your canine to turn out to be increasingly expressive when he feels the desire – correspondence that is as useful to us all things considered to our mutts.

Second, when we get him in the demonstration we can give quick input. A basic "Hello, hello!" while hustling him to his potty spot will point out that there's a contrast between the spot where he began and that extraordinary spot you need him to go.

While housetraining another pooch (pup or grown-up) I ensure I comprehend what my canine considers "platinum level prizes." Housetraining is a serious deal, and it necessitates that we recognize our canine's prosperity with a fitting result for their accomplishment. High-esteem nourishment prizes ought to be put away on a rack or table by the entryway so you can snatch them in transit out with your pooch. What's more, the prizes of applause and have ought to be plentifully impact of the potty party that commends your canine's prosperity at pottying in the best possible spot.

Housetraining Regression

It is troubling when you think housetraining has been accomplished, just to discover inappropriately found puddles or craps. Here are a few reasons your pooch's housetraining may unwind:

Urinary tract diseases or other restorative concerns can bring about potty mishaps. In the event that your completely housetrained hound starts to potty in the house, your first stop ought to be your veterinarian. Physical issues must be precluded before accepting the issue is a conduct one. Before your visit, evaluate your canine's water and nourishment admission so you can report any progressions that may be a piece of the image.

Perceive that a canine's housetraining may not move to new situations. I have had numerous customers whose canines' housetraining self-destructed when visiting the home of a companion, after a move, or even in an open spot (how humiliating!).

Because a canine is housetrained in one condition doesn't mean he is housetrained in all situations. At the point when you change conditions, accept your pooch isn't housetrained until you have helped your canine comprehend that the propensities learned in one spot can likewise apply to the new setting. To do this, return your canine to Housetraining 101.Regular difficulties. Similarly as your canine may need to relearn housetraining in another condition, so may he have to relearn housetraining in various seasons. I have had numerous customers find that their late spring doggy's housetraining disentangled at the main fall downpour or winter day off.

I generally encourage customers to be proactive climate watchers. In the event that your pooch's potty spot is outside, think about that potty propensities can and may change with the season, and you may need to consider inventive and proactive approaches to keep your canine's potty propensities solid. For hounds who hate downpour, the erection of a versatile shelter may very well facilitate the torment. A snow scoop goes far in helping little pooches manage profound day off. Some indoor-open air floor covering can support the warmth of summer asphalt.

Separate between assuaging oneself and checking. Stamping conduct can create in hounds after their housetraining is finished up, as pooches develop and hormonal levels change. Checking is a characteristic conduct of both male and female pooches, however increasingly articulated in male mutts. I approach checking like all housetraining issues, returning pooches to Housetraining 101, with the accentuation on sharp consideration, since it is essential to intrude on the desire to stamp before genuine house-ruining happens. For hounds who are ceaseless markers, a tummy band that forestalls house-ruining might be a useful administration device.

Think about dread or tension being a contributing component. One of my customers was alarmed when her Newfoundland began pottying in the house. As it turned out, the canine was pottying inside in light of the fact that he had gotten terrified of wandering into his yard following a neighbor's house being re-roofed. The torrent of impacts from the nailer had so damaged the poor canine that he got housebound, leaving him no decision yet to potty in the house, bringing on additional uneasiness.

For this situation, we built up an indoor potty zone that was utilized while we took a shot at revamping positive relationship with his patio condition.

Potty Problems that are NOT Housetraining Problems

Automatic pee and poo can happen for various reasons with the shared factor to all being that the pooch just has no influence over it. Here are some normal explanations behind automatic pottying:

Energy pee. A few canines, particularly youthful pooches, will automatically create a puddle during glad homecomings and other blissful circumstances. Since most trigger circumstances can be anticipated, the most ideal approach to lessen energy pee is to make light of welcome and other sincerely charged circumstances by overlooking or just coolly welcoming your canine.

It likewise at times gives your pooch another thing to do at the times when he is energized. For instance, you may enter your home with one of your canine's toys close by, hurl it away from you, stroll past your pooch while he recovers it, at that point welcome your canine a few minutes after the fact once the underlying energy worn off. Since the trigger for energy pee is a huge arrangement to the canine, it's useful to set up and practice mock welcome over and again so the trigger turns out to be less energizing – maybe even a bit of exhausting.

Compliant pee. This type of automatic pee is about social signs. It happens when your pooch's passionate response to a trigger (e.g., a more odd or a relative) is one of settlement, maybe even dread. Compliant pee can be upsetting to loved ones who trigger it; they may think it proposes they have been compromising or horrible toward the canine, in any event, when they have not. As a rule, the canine might be reacting to the human's body stance and size, voice volume and tone, or different qualities that trigger an inborn agreeable reaction.

Compliant pee issues can be frequently be settled by making light of welcome, counter-molding the nearness of the individual (constructing a positive passionate relationship with the trigger), training people who trigger the agreeable pee to stay away from provocative non-verbal communication, (for example, direct eye to eye connection with the pooch, approaching over or going after him, direct frontal methodologies, and noisy non-verbal communication and voices).

Against Icky Poo by Mister Max

I have additionally discovered that showing the canine a signal that implies somebody is going to approach, (for example, "Hi, I'm Here!") can lessen compliant pee by expelling the component of shock from the collaborations.

Incontinence. Age and disease can deliver urinary and additionally fecal incontinence in our pooches. Sick or old pooches may spill pee or oust dung while resting or may encounter abrupt desires to potty and be not able make it out the entryway. Female pooches with hormonal changes may spill pee, as well. While numerous individuals acknowledge incontinence as an unavoidable piece of their pooches' wellbeing or maturing, both western and eastern prescription offer cures, so a visit to your veterinarian is an absolute necessity. The utilization of midsection groups, doggie undies, and potty cushions in dozing territories may help diminish the weights of tidy up.

Basic Tools for Housetraining

It makes the entire housetraining task a million times simpler on the off chance that you are set up ahead of time of your new canine or doggy's appearance with every one of the things you should deal with his whereabouts and bolster his advancement. Here are the basics:

A carton, versatile exercise pen, or little room furnished with an infant entryway, so you can make a proper restriction territory for your canine. This will keep undesirable mishaps from happening. Forestalling undesirable mishaps guarantees our mutts don't practice pottying in improper places and prevents the non-potty spots from turning out to be implanted with those potty aromas that can trigger a pooch into committing an error. Some great tidy up items to dispose of potty scents from your home should a mishap occur (as it may, since we're just human and we do commit errors). While there are numerous available and plans for potty tidy up creations can be discovered on the web, my undisputed top choice is unscented Anti-Icky Poo by Mister Max (accessible in some pet stock stores and on the web). It contains proteins that help annihilate the scent causing mixes in pee.

A prepared inventory of significant level (as characterized by the canine) compensations to dole out to your pooch when the person in question hits the nail on the head. Proper pottying is anything but a lowest pay permitted by law action; think of it as a canine demonstration of virtuoso when your new pooch gets pottying right and compensation with the stuff (nourishment treats, toys, and play) that your pooch truly values.

Now and again, potty cushions might be useful, however I for one want to reject them from my housetraining conventions (it's one less advance to become dim to get to the last objective of the pooch pottying in a particular spot).

For a few, it's useful to make an indoor can zone – a litter box for hounds, in a manner of speaking. In the event that an indoor latrine zone for your canine would be useful for you, the "litterbox" should be accessible as a potty goal as it so happens. In cases including pee stamping, paunch groups can be a useful apparatus. They don't fore-stall stamping however they do forestall house dirtying, and numerous mutts appear to cease from checking when the stomach band is on. Paunch groups are accessible in different sizes from pet stock stores and on the web.

Potty Pads for House Training?

I am not an aficionado of presenting potty cushions as a component of a housetraining system. On the off chance that the objective of housetraining is for your pooch to potty outside, at that point potty cushions make a center advance that must in the end be eliminated as a major aspect of the general housetraining plan. I would prefer to begin concentrating a pooch's consideration promptly on the last goal. Why make an additional progression on the off chance that we don't need to?

A few people, be that as it may, plan for their pooches to have an indoor toileting spot, with potty cushions as a feature of their canines' deep rooted situation. This can be helpful, so you don't need to make that excursion outside, by giving a canine a legitimate potty spot inside. Be that as it may, they don't mystically pull in pooches to take out on them; hounds should be instructed to utilize them, much the same as they should be educated to go outside. Either undertaking can be practiced by adhering to the principles of house preparing 101.

Individuals in some cases choose to utilize potty cushions since they need to disregard their pooches inside for longer timeframes than their mutts can hold it. If so with your pooch, ensure you leave her in a bigger long haul control zone than the previously mentioned containers or comfortable repression zone. Make a region for dozing and hanging out, and a different space for disposing of on the potty cushions.

· · ·

weewee cushions for hounds

Pooch Doors: Yay or Nay?

As the glad watchman of both a shiny new Aussie little dog and an "abrupt urge" Greyhound senior, I am thankful for my pooch entryway. My pooches go in and out voluntarily, never expecting to approach me to utilize my opposable thumb to turn the handle to open that entryway. At my home, there's no compelling reason to locate the chaperon to get the bathroom key; the restroom entryway is constantly opened. My canines go out, my mutts come in. There's nary a potty mishap or stress.

doorbell for hound

(Note: Some individuals stress over things that can happen to their canines outside in their yards if the pooch is unattended. The yard that is accessible to my mutts through my canine entryway is super pooch sealed and twofold fenced. All things considered, there are a greater number of threats to an unattended canine outside than inside, yet this is a hazard I have taken with my pooches for a long time without an issue. You may settle on an alternate decision.)

No ifs, ands or buts, my new little guy has figured out how to go outside to potty and I am excited that she has figured out how to utilize the pooch entryway. At the point when nature gets she jumps through and out. There hasn't been a mishap in weeks and I'm free as entryway orderly. Be that as it may, is my new pup completely house-trained? The appropriate response is... no!

. . .

Other than realizing where to potty, our mutts need to figure out how to "hold it" when they can't gain admittance to the potty spot. What's more, they have to figure out how to educate us that they need our assistance to get from here to there. Without these exercises, house-training is inadequate and potty incidents will undoubtedly happen when hound entryways aren't accessible – maybe when the canine entryway is accidentally left shut or when we're visiting the home of a pooch entryway lacking companion.

My new puppy will go with me soon and I don't think the pooch amicable inn has a canine entryway (that is a piece excessively agreeable). I would be wise to start Housetraining 101, as opposed to letting my canine entryway permit me take the lethargic way out. Also, as an extra to the fundamental preparing, I'll be showing my new little guy to ring a "Hello, I gotta go!" ringer. It's entirely easy to prepare a pooch to ring a bell (I think about this as a call for room administration) and regarding my educated reaction (bounce up and take care of her), I'm a quite fast investigation. (For guidelines on showing a canine to ring a bell on the entryway, see "Target-Train Your Dog to Ring A Doorbell".)

Appropriate House Training is A Great Investment of Time

This may all stable like a huge amount of work; it isn't really so. On the off chance that you watch the CRAP rules (Confinement, Routine, Attention, and Platinum rewards) from the absolute first day with your new pooch or little guy, he ought to rapidly make sense of when and where to "go" (maybe on prompt!), and how to "hold it" at all different occasions. His prosperity at these errands may represent the moment of truth your satisfaction at living respectively, so give it your absolute best!

Instructions to House-Train A Puppy: Problem-Solving

Golden was a sweetheart Golden Retriever little guy who had moved on from my Puppy Kindergarten with distinction. She had a solid establishment in socialization and preparing, which had brought about her having a glad and positive perspective and great little dog habits. Above all, Amber had aced housetraining. At the hour of her graduation, her folks gladly noticed that Amber had not pottied in the house in weeks, and when she needed to go, she let her folks know by crying at the entryway.

I next got notification from Amber's mother when Amber was barely a half year old. Totally surprisingly, Amber had begun peeing in the house! While the peeing was issue number one, a subsequent issue was that Amber had begun to disregard her proprietors and appeared to be commonly progressively "crazy." The presence of these two practices together drove her father to one end: Amber's unseemly peeing, alongside her obliviousness and raucousness, all coming at this high school minute, was evidence positive that she needed to apply her predominance on her family. Goodness, kid. I had another idea that I imparted to Amber's mother: When a completely house-trained hound begins peeing as well as pooping in the house, one must get thee and thine canine to a veterinarian to preclude a medicinal reason! Urinary tract contaminations are a typical explanation that an in the past housetrained pooch may begin peeing in the house; the difficult condition causes a criticalness that couple of canines can stand up to.

Sufficiently sure, Amber's therapeutic stir up indicated only that. After a course of anti-toxins – and her proprietors' recharged preparing practice sessions – Amber's "strength issue" completely vanished.

Latrine preparing for little dogs: essential tips and methods

Step by step instructions to latrine train your pooch

Can preparing your pup ought to be a significant basic procedure, as long as you take the time and inconvenience to get into a decent daily practice.

At first, you should manufacture your daily practice around your little dog's needs, and these are dependably unsurprising when they are extremely youthful. Little dogs need to pee following awakening, so you should be there to bring your pup straight into the nursery immediately.

Eating its dinner animates its stomach related framework, and doggies ordinarily pee inside fifteen minutes of eating, and crap inside 30 minutes of eating (in spite of the fact that this may differ somewhat with every person).

Pups have poor bladder control, and need to pee no less than consistently or two. They can pee suddenly when they get energized, so take your little dog out habitually on the off chance that it has been dynamic, playing or investigating.

You may think that its helpful to track when your doggy eats rests, pees and poos. A basic journal rundown will do. Rehash sign words like 'small wees' and 'crap craps' or 'be occupied' and 'be spotless' while the doggy is really peeing or pooping. Utilize various words for each activity so you will have the option to provoke the little dog later on.

Continuously go with your little dog into the nursery so you are there to remunerate and append the prompt words to the fruitful activities! Luckily, little dogs are animals of propensity, so as long as you acquaint the nursery with your pup as its latrine region right off the bat, you ought to have the option to maintain a strategic distance from the majority of the normal entanglements.

Step by step instructions to can prepare your little dog: normal blunders

Lamentably there are numerous reasons why 'can preparing' probably won't go as easily as possible, so ensure you don't commit any of the accompanying errors:

- Over-encouraging.
- Encouraging an unacceptable eating routine or giving an assortment of nourishments.
- Not encouraging at customary occasions.

Bolstering at an inappropriate occasions (which could cause medium-term crap).

Rebuffing the little dog for its indoor mishaps (which can make it terrified of toileting before you - even outside). Nourishing salty nourishments (for example stock from 3D squares) which makes them drink more.

Utilizing alkali based cleaning mixes (which smell like pee).

Anticipating that the little dog should reveal to you when it needs to go out; this is unreasonable, so it is smarter to take them out at customary interims.

Welcoming the little dog to go back and forth however it sees fit (doggy will believe that the nursery is an undertaking play area, as opposed to a can territory. Additionally, what is a doggy intended to do when the climate gets cold, and it is looked with a shut secondary passage?).

Leaving the pup alone excessively long, with the goal that it is compelled to go inside (which sets an awful point of reference, or even a propensity for going inside). Erroneously partner the words 'great young lady' or 'great kid' when they latrine, instead of the particular signal words. Think about what could happen whenever you acclaim your canine?

Access to mats or floor covering (which are pleasant and retentive - simply like grass).

Lethargy on your part, bringing about a greater number of wees inside than outside.

Disregarding the doggy in the nursery, so you are not there to compensate it for going outside... how is it intended to discover that it is increasingly mainstream and invaluable going outside, in the event that you are not there to show your endorsement? Agreeable or energized pee on welcome (if this happens, take your little dog outside before you welcome it and tone down your welcome so it is less energizing or overpowering).

It is unjustifiable to anticipate that your pup should go directly during that time when it is youthful.

Dozing the little dog in a container or doggy pen can help with house preparing yet you should let it out in the nursery to diminish itself during the night.

You are here: Home/Dog Training/5 Simple Tips For Potty Training Your Puppy

5 Simple Tips for Potty Training Your Puppy

In the late 90's I found a fairly straightforward approach to potty train a pup, and it worked so well I've been utilizing it from that point forward. Following seven days of utilizing these tips you'll take out 90% of mishaps, and you'll be well while in transit to a having a completely house prepared little guy.

This procedure works by being forestalling mishaps before they occur, and by showing your canine that going potty outside is the best thing ever.

Since potty preparing is a progressing procedure I've separated this article into fourteen day sections. The primary week is the place the potty preparing enchantment occurs, and the subsequent week is the place the consistency of week one begins to pay off. Here's 5 straightforward tips for potty preparing your little dog.

The First Week of Potty Training Your Puppy

The primary seven day stretch of potty preparing a little dog is incredibly tiring, I'm not going to mislead anybody. Yet, I guarantee it gets simpler. You may wind up addressing why you settled on a pup in any case — trust me, we've all been there. Be that as it may, after the principal week you'll have the option to loosen up more, and you'll begin to perceive how well your consistency pays off.

. . .

The principal week is the place you will keep a close eye on your puppy, ensuring you mediate before any mishaps occur. During the main week you're going to should know where your little guy is consistently.

1. Focus on Your Puppy At All Times

A calm little dog is inconvenience, or so the expression goes. Regardless of whether he's getting into the trash, eating your new shoes or crapping over in the corner — a calm doggy signals inconvenience.

On the off chance that you need to forestall mishaps before they happen you're going to need to watch your little guy consistently, including each time they stray. It just takes one mishap to slow down your preparation. Presently I realize that viewing your pup relentless isn't actually fun and energizing, however having the option to get them before they have a mishap is the reason this technique works so well.

In case you're similar to me and experience difficulty staying aware of your little guy consistently have a go at utilizing a tie. You can purchase a tie from the pet store or basically do what I did and utilize a long lead or rope. In the event that tying your little guy to you consistently is the stuff to ensure they're not sneaking off then put it all on the line. In case you're not excited about keeping your pooch fastened you can utilize infant entryways or shut ways to confine your canines access to the entire house.

2. Try not to Leave Your Puppy Unattended

Did I notice the significance of not letting your pooch far out? I did, yet this part is so significant I have to make reference to it twice. Your activity when house preparing is to be there to forestall mishaps before they occur. You know when your pooch will have a mishap? The minute you're not looking. There's very little you can do that bodes well after your pooch has had a mishap — and you've passed up a significant preparing exercise.

Try not to rebuff your canine in the event that they pee inside.

Notwithstanding every one of those old preparing thoughts discipline is certainly not a decent hindrance for house preparing. Hollering at your canine sometime later just befuddles them and makes them anxious around you. On the off chance that you get your did in the demonstration you can attempt to stand out enough to be noticed and move them outside. In case you're fruitful and they keep going once you get outside commendation them like there's no tomorrow.

Your little guy will have a mishap or two in the house – there's no way to avoid it. What you can do is keep them from having more by being proactive. Keep them in your sight consistently and take them out each time they begin to stray.

3. Let Your Dog Out Once Every Hour or Two

Letting your little guy outside consistently or two gets old, however it's the least complex approach to keep mishaps from occurring. In the event that you've at any point asked why a few people decide to get new little dogs throughout the late spring or when they're on an extended get-away it most likely has to do with potty preparing. In the event that you've house preparing a canine before you know how much time and responsibility it takes.

Here and there your canine probably won't pee outside and that is OK. An inefficient outside time is superior to a mishap inside. Let them meander around a tad and head back inside.

Despite the fact that most canines can deal with staying asleep for the entire evening without mishaps remember that their bladders are terribly little so on the off chance that you can abstain from snoozing I'd do as such. Most doggies can't hold it for that long. To forestall medium-term mishaps ensure your puppy has peed before sleep time.

4. Recognition Your Dog Like There's No Tomorrow

Each time your canine pees or craps outside it should be commended. Give them infant talk or a treat, hop up and down, pat their little heads and help them to remember how splendid that choice was. Truly it may look senseless, however your little guy has to realize he's done the best thing ever. At the point when you reliably acclaim your doggy for going potty outside they'll begin to comprehend that it's the right choice, and one that prompts overly fun cheerful time. Also, with regards to commend don't think little of how persuading it is with regards to getting your puppy to rehash attractive practices. Utilizing acclaim is an unmistakable method to tell your pooch that they're making the best decision at the correct minute, and with redundancy they'll begin figuring "I ought to go potty outside in light of the fact that that satisfies everybody."

The Second Week of Potty Training Your Puppy

This is the 'keep it up' period where the commendation is still substantial however you can loosen up somewhat more with regards to watching your little guy.

5. Keep Up The Praise and Watch For Signals

Try not to get languid with the acclaim during the subsequent week. You need your pooch to be the proudest animal on earth each time he pees or craps outside. Truly it appears to be senseless inevitably, and possibly somewhat dreadful if your canine gazes at you while doing their business – however have confidence, you're getting the message over.

Tell your canine that peeing and crapping outside is marvelous, and that a wide range of extraordinary things come to little guys that do magnificent things.

In spite of the fact that it varies by every individual pooch this is when most will think of their own little method for telling you they must go. It may be crying at your feet, ringing a bell you've set up or holding up at the entryway — simply make certain to focus on these signs and development. When your pooch realizes how to stand out enough to be noticed when he must go you can loosen up a little and praise yourself on a vocation all around done.

Instructions to Potty Train Your Dog

Rapid, solid potty preparing may be the most widely recognized solicitation of each new little dog proprietor. In spite of the fact that potty preparing is a direct procedure at its center, it very well may be loaded up with disarray, misconception and dissatisfaction. Yet, never dread! You and your little dog can ace the potty preparing process by following these means and tips.

Strategies for Potty Training

There is just a single adequate procedure for potty preparing a pooch of all ages: uplifting feedback. Customary counsel proposed swatting a canine or focusing all over his loss for botches in the house, however those strategies do nothing to make the potty preparing process progressively justifiable for your pooch and can really harm your association with him. Remember, hounds don't see their waste the manner in which we do – to them, pee and crap is entirely intriguing! Rebuffing your pooch for going in the house won't enable him to comprehend what he ought to do rather and might make him hesitant to go close to you by any means, inside or out. Fruitful potty preparing requires tolerance, thoughtfulness and recollecting that your new little dog is simply learning the guidelines.

Carton preparing is an incredible method to begin your little dog off on the correct paw. Canines have a characteristic intuition to keep their sanctum clean, so an appropriately measured case, presented step by step, will make a command post for your little dog and will prevent him from having mishaps when you can't watch him. Utilize the case when you can't give your doggy your complete consideration during the day, just as at snooze time and sleep time. Choosing the correct size carton is basic, and it ought to be sufficiently large so your little dog can easily stand up, pivot and rests yet very little greater. On the off chance that you settle on a carton that is excessively enormous, your little dog will have the option to potty in one corner and rest easily in the other, invalidating the point of box preparing.

While indoor disposal arrangements like potty cushions and litter boxes have their place, utilizing them can in reality moderate the procedure down on the off chance that you plan to in the long run have your canine dispense with only outside. Showing your little dog to potty inside now and again and outside others can be confounding on the grounds that you will in the long run need to show your canine that sooner or later the indoor alternative is never again permitted. Potty cushions work best for individuals who can't get their pup outside rapidly, similar to the individuals who live in skyscraper lofts or have constrained portability.

Setting a Potty Training Schedule

Pooches flourish with an anticipated calendar, and setting one up for your new doggy will make life simpler for both of you. Feed your little dog at similar occasions every day to assist you with foreseeing and timetable restroom breaks. Timetable post-supper strolls, just as hourly outings outside during the underlying phases of potty preparing. Continuously take your pup out subsequent to crating, regardless of whether was uniquely for a brief span, and recall that energetic play ought to consistently be hindered for potty breaks. Probably the greatest mix-up new doggy proprietors make is anticipating that their little dog should hold it for longer than he is physically fit. The general rule for doggy "hold times" is that every period of age likens to an hour of "hold time," so a two-month-old pup can hold it for around two hours. There are exemptions to the standard; your little dog ought to have the option to hold it for marginally longer timeframe around evening time as he gets more established and you puppy will require potty breaks all the more as often as possible when he's playing.

Apparatuses Needed for Potty Training

You'll need to have the accompanying things as you start potty preparing your pooch:

An appropriately estimated container: a box will guard your little dog when you can't watch him and assist him with figuring out how to hold it as a result of his craving to keep his lair clean.

A chain: regardless of whether you have a fenced-in yard, take your little dog out on a rope with the goal that he isn't enticed to play rather than potty. A rope will likewise enable you to be sufficiently close to your little dog to remunerate him following end.

Treats: giving your pooch a little treat following he potties will instruct him that he gets remunerated for going in the correct spot.

Child entryway: infant doors are an incredible method to ward your doggy from sneaking off to different pieces of the house unaided. Stain and scent remover: utilizing the correct sort of cleaner will keep your doggy from searching out spots that he's as of now filthy.

Taking Your Dog Outside

Perhaps the simplest approaches to forestall mishaps is figuring out how to perceive when your doggy needs to go out. Most little dogs will sniff the ground when they're preparing to potty, however there are numerous other more signals that occur before sniffing. Pups that pace, appear to be diverted and leave play are unpretentiously flagging that they need to go out. On the off chance that your little dog attempts to escape the room, enjoy a potty reprieve immediately.

You ought to consistently go with your little dog outside for potty breaks. You're there not exclusively to guarantee that he really goes, you're additionally there to remunerate your doggy with a treat for going in the best possible spot. Hold up until your doggy completes the process of killing and quickly give him a delicious compensation for a vocation very much done. On the off chance that you hold up until you get back in the house, your doggy won't make the association between his disposal and the prize. It likewise shows your little dog a "potty expression" when you take him outside for a restroom break. A potty expression is an approach to tenderly remind your pup what he needs to do when he's outside. It's a major assistance during the potty preparing period of puppyhood and you can keep on utilizing for an incredible remainder. Pick an expression like "hustle just a bit" or "feel free to" state it delicately directly as your pup disposes of. In time your pooch will connect the expression with the demonstration of disposal, so you can say it when your doggy gets occupied and overlooks what he needs to do outside.

PHYSICAL AND MENTAL EXERCISES FOR YOUR DOG AND BREED SELECTION

CHAPTER 3

Games to Exercise Your Dog's Body and Mind

As of late, an understudy came to class griping that she had taken her two-year-old Labrador Retriever for a three-mile run, at that point left to get her child from school, and when she got back she found that her pooch had destroyed two love seat pads and was really busy biting the leg off her kitchen seat. That equivalent week, another understudy deplored that when she returned home from the market in the wake of completing an effective 30-minute instructional meeting with her Rottweiler, she found that he had torn up his new case tangle, at that point pulled the curtains off the window and into his case, and was tearing them to pieces. So what was the issue? Shouldn't the Labrador have been physically depleted and the Rottweiler intellectually depleted? Truly and yes. Be that as it may, the way to progress is in destroying them both physically and intellectually. Everything necessary is a bit of arranging. Start with playing these two games, and afterward have a go at making up your very own portion.

Preparing Game 1: Wild Sits

The most effective method to play: Taught when a canine comprehends the idea of "sit," Wild Sits starts by having the pooch on chain while the proprietor goes around cheering, bouncing all over, and getting the canine irritated up. (Note: If a pooch is docile, apprehensive, or touchy, mitigate the ferocity. The objective is an energized, not alarmed pooch.) Then, mid-cavort, the proprietor will teach the canine to sit. (This should be possible with a treat if the pooch is a pup or new to preparing.) He most likely won't comply with the first run through or two, however after a little practice, he'll have the option to go from acting hyper to sitting quietly on direction.

The advantages: Besides the cardio exercise you and your pooch are getting during this activity, you're showing your canine to hear you out while he's in a condition of hyperactivity. How regularly has your canine gone crazy when the doorbell rings or when he sees individuals in the city and disregarded your arguing for him to sit? Presently you're showing him how to pull himself once more into a responsive and submissive perspective. How extraordinary is that?

Preparing Game 2: Cardio Twist

Step by step instructions to play: Those who know about the game of deftness realize this activity as weave shafts, however any canine proprietor can show her pet to do it as an approach to have some good times, chip away at coordination, and get a cardio exercise. Essentially set up "shafts" utilizing collapsing seats, orange cones, unused latrine uncloggers, or even individuals, and educate your canine to heel close by you as you weave between them, changing your pace from quick to slow. Consider it being like a slalom course in skiing.

The advantages: Your canine needs to focus more diligently on tailing you as you rapidly alter course. Additionally, on the grounds that he'll remain at your left side as you rapidly weave left and right, he'll need to alter his pace to be increasingly slow, separately, which is the thing that your fitness coach would call interim preparing. Include considerably all the more an exercise by running the whole course.

Give exchanging a shot one of your ordinary instructional courses with these games. Notwithstanding having a well-prepared and well-practiced pooch, you will likewise receive the rewards of getting more cardio. And keeping in mind that I'm not proposing this can be an option in contrast to heading off to the rec center, I am talking as a matter of fact that by doing this, your association with your pooch and with your own physicality will improve significantly.

Enhancing Your Dog's Life

Weariness and abundance vitality are two normal explanations behind conduct issues in hounds. This bodes well since they're intended to have dynamic existences. Wild canines spend about 80% of their waking hours chasing and rummaging for nourishment. Residential canines have been aiding and working nearby us for a great many years, and most are reproduced for a particular reason, for example, chasing, cultivating or security. For instance, retrievers and pointers were reared to find and bring game and water fowls. Fragrance dogs, similar to coonhounds and beagles, were reproduced to discover bunnies, foxes and other little prey. Canines like German shepherds, collies, steers mutts and sheepdogs were reproduced to group domesticated animals. Regardless of whether canines were working for us or rummaging alone, their endurance once relied upon heaps of activity and critical thinking. Be that as it may, shouldn't something be said about at this point?

Today that is altogether changed. Presently the most well-known set of working responsibilities for hounds is Couch Potato! While we're away at work throughout the day, they rest. Also, when we get back home, we serve them free nourishment in a bowl—no exertion required from them. They eat a bigger number of calories than they can utilize. The outcome is hounds who are exhausted senseless, frequently overweight and have an excess of vitality. It's an ideal formula for conduct issues.

What Does Your Dog Need?

It's not important to leave your place of employment, take up duck chasing or get yourself a lot of sheep to keep your canine out of difficulty. Be that as it may, we urge you to discover approaches to practice her cerebrum and body. Peruse on for some fun, down to earth approaches to enhance your pooch's life, both when you're near and when you're most certainly not. You'll see that these thoughts go far toward keeping your pooch glad and simpler to live with. Evaluate a couple and see what you and your canine appreciate most.

Tips for Alone Time

Since we as a whole have occupied existences, our pooches regularly wind up spending a decent part of their day home alone. In the event that you give your canine "occupations" to do when she's without anyone else's input, she'll be more averse to think of her own particular manners to involve her time, such as unstuffing your sofa, assaulting the garbage or biting on your preferred pair of shoes. Furthermore, she'll be more averse to energetically handle you when you get back home, after she's gone through a day sitting idle however energizing her batteries!

6 Great Ways To Challenge Your Dog's Mind

Much the same as individuals, hounds get exhausted with the regular old ordinary everyday practice. Keeping them slow-witted and continually presenting them to new things is similarly as significant as going for them for strolls and practicing them. Exhausted canines create damaging practices and take their negative vitality out on things like your furnishings.

Here are some inventive approaches to animate your pooch's psyche so they don't get exhausted and get rowdy:

1. Work on another stunt

Each time you draw in your canine in an instructional course, you are furnishing him with a psychological test. Quest around for new deceives to chip away at. In case you're prepared to move past the fundamental directions, look at books, check the Internet, and approach a mentor for thoughts for new deceives and preparing thoughts.

"My canine, Vince just as of late turned 4-years of age and I at last selected him in acquiescence school. It has changed both our lives. Presently on days where I work him on new deceives and such, I have seen that his personality has quieted down. Testing him intellectually makes him significantly less restless when all is said in done and he has gotten progressively loose around different canines. Vince is evidence that old canines can adapt new deceives." – Sara Hicks

2. Play with intelligent games or plays with your canine

Buy a doggie table game or a canine riddle to challenge your little guy. Draw in your pooch in a round of Dog Memory or Dog Dominos. Give your pooch one of the many toys that enable you to shroud treats and items inside and draw in your canine to make sense of how to function them out. "This sounds senseless however I purchased this prepackaged game that I saw at the store for my pooch Snickers and I to play together. I put treats underneath a peg and she needs to make sense of which ones to lift up so as to discover where the treats are. There is another adaptation where I conceal the treats with this bit of plastic and Snickers needs to turn the board around to reveal the treats. It truly challenges her and I see her cerebrum endeavoring to make sense of everything." – Donna Marr

3. Get things done with your canine

Indeed, even a fast race to the letter box, a stopover at a companion's home, or a turn through the vehicle wash will put your pooch up close and personal with an assortment of energizers.

"Indeed, even simply taking Ryker for a vehicle ride or to the vehicle wash is animating for him. He gets the opportunity to see loads of various sights and sounds and experience new circumstances. He cherishes proceeding to get so energized. What's more, I can see his cerebrum functioning as it takes it all in. What's more, when we get back home, he falls right snoozing, despite the fact that it wasn't physically saddling." – Jennifer Brody

4. Give your pooch a vocation to do

Mutts are reared to finish assignments, for example, chasing and grouping. At the point when they aren't ready to satisfy these kinds of obligations, they can get eager. Draw in your pooch in a round of Frisbee. Get him associated with a game like nimbleness or Flyball. Take him for a long walk, climb, or swim. Secure positions that satisfy your canine's breed. In the event that you have a retriever, for instance, nothing will leave it more fulfilled than a healthy round of get.

"I can take my pooch for a walk or a run, yet what truly makes her the most joyful is a generous round of get. I take a tennis racket to the canine park and hit a ball the extent that I can. She will take it back to me again and again like it's her activity." – John Kurmai

5. Acquaint your pooch with new faces

Each time your pooch meets another individual or individual canine, they are acquainted with new sights, sounds, and butts to sniff. Taking you little guy to places like the pooch park will furnish him with sufficient chance to connect with his detects. "I every now and again take Bruiser to the canine park, which he completely adores! Bruiser always meets new companions there and discovers individuals to sniff and get petted by. This has truly caused him to listen better, less on edge and genuinely increasingly fulfilled." – Kat Malkowych

6. Give them new toys and pivot out the old ones

You wouldn't have any desire to play with something very similar consistently would you? At that point you shouldn't anticipate that your canine should keep on adoring a similar toy that he's had for a considerable length of time. Give him a toy to play with for a couple of days and when he becomes exhausted of it, supplant it with another.

"Moogly has such huge numbers of toys yet at the same time gets exhausted. It's crazy! I am continually bringing new toys into the house however he has a limited capacity to focus so they just keep him engaged for some time. We began keeping the entirety of his toys in a canister in the storage room and pivoting them out. He has such a significant number of now and we'll switch up another toy with one that he's had for quite a long time and that he may have disregarded. He adores this and at whatever point we switch them up, he is similarly as energized as when he gets a spic and span toy." – Katie Adams

Keep Your Dog Mentally And Physically Fit

So as to be balanced pets, hounds need both mental and physical incitement every day. The longing to "keep occupied" is profoundly imbued in most of canines.

Working, chasing, crowding and guarding breeds are by all account not the only ones with this need. Indeed, even little types of pooches hold a specific measure of hard working attitude for instance, a Yorkie with bows in its hair is as yet a terrier, and their proprietors realize that these minor folks still appreciate terrier-type practices, for example, pursuing and burrowing. If not given an outlet for their vitality, pooches of any size can get dangerous, on edge or baffled, causing various conduct issues.

Getting Your Dog The Exercise He Or She Needs

So what amount does practice does your canine genuinely need? There's no solid answer, however enough exercise to feel really worn out. Most solid pooches will profit by practice sessions in both the morning and the night. A safe, fenced region for off-chain practice is perfect, yet on the off chance that you don't approach this, snap a rope on your little guy and take a walk.

Except if your canine has an ailment requiring constrained exercise, at that point make at any rate one of your pooch's trips a vigorous action. Playing with different pooches off-rope in a fenced zone, swimming, playing bring or running adjacent to a jogger are altogether amazing oxygen consuming activities. Continuously make certain to watch out for your puppy to look for exhaustion and ensure your pooch approaches cool water and shade whenever they are working out.

A few people even train their mutts to run on a treadmill. You can begin with only a couple of moments, and step by step work up to a brief treadmill practice session. Exercise of this nature will discharge endorphins which will have a general quieting impact on your pooch's conduct, just as numerous other medical advantages.

Little dog Safe Activities

Exercises appropriate for grown-up canines may not be alright for developing young doggies. Playing is the best decision for a more youthful puppy, regardless of whether it's off-chain with different canines, playing get or different games with their human. Set up play dates with companions so your little guy can learn social abilities and get some activity.

Running or biking on asphalt are undependable activities for youthful mutts whose bones are not full fledged. On the off chance that you have any inquiries concerning whether a specific sort of activity is alright for your doggy, check with your veterinarian. Continuously check with your veterinarian.

Remember mental incitement! Instructional courses keep a canine's mind sharp, just as help create and reinforce the bond among pooch and human. Abstain from exhausting or dreary exercises. Make it fun! Work on instructing your canine stunts like sit and remain alongside basic spryness works out. Short instructional courses are ideal, mixed with play or rest sessions and bunches of acclaim and love.

Step by step instructions to Tire out a Puppy: 4 Exercises That'll Have Him Behaving in No Time

We are pulled in by work (frequently taking a few employments just to make a decent living), family, internet based life, interests and ordinarily we simply don't set aside a few minutes for our mutts. Indeed, even I work all day with a couple of employments of late! Also, I have high drive hounds that need a great deal of activity.

Mental Stimulation

Tackling riddles and utilizing your psyche is depleting. Try not to trust me? Take a school class or go to a proceeding with instruction class for a day or two.

Get familiar with some new data. What's more, attempt and disclose to me you are not worn out when you are finished! Except if obviously you are utilized to consistent adapting each day. On the off chance that you need a drained canine, show him something new, or if nothing else put a turn on the things that he knows by drawing in his brain.

Try not to adhere to the equivalent careful preparing routine with your little guy every day, in a similar exhausting request.

Blend things up, cause him to perform quicker and make it a game. Mental incitement is likewise pivotal to his joy. Dr. Ian Dunbar (one of my preferred behaviorists) says that psychological exercise tires a pooch physically more than physical exercise does!

That is amazing stuff! Canines need compliance preparing. They need sports. They need riddles and games. Also, even things to bite on can here and there animate them intellectually. Recollect in past articles, me insinuating not enabling your baby to work out? Presently envision not enabling your baby to play or learn or animate his brain. Would you be able to envision? No books, no toys, next to no verbal collaboration or educating.

That would be brutal. Canines, too, need to ever be invigorated intellectually.

In the event that we don't give it to them through physical and verbal association and learning and compensating great conduct, our pooch will give it to themselves through biting and destroying and yapping and burrowing and bouncing and acting a blockhead. Hyper pooch or high vitality hounds are frequently intellectually more insightful than their partners. They are not satisfied sitting and playing bring with a couple toys or chewies.

They ought to be shown mental activities and games! Actually it doesn't make a difference what you instruct them:

- Fundamental Obedience
- Middle of the road Obediencedog games
- Propelled Obedience
- Dexterity
- Motivation Control Games
- Stunts
- Administration Commands

Or then again even a hand stand up the divider…

Interestingly, you are instructing and giving that psychological incitement that will fulfill them!

#3 HIIT Exercise

Have you at any point done H.I.I.T or High Intensity Interval Training? Those are four of my most noticeably terrible feared words when they are hung together in a sentence. I am right now getting go into shape and figuring out how to deadlift, squat, and seat press securely. My fitness coach has faith in HIIT preparing and draws in me both with weight preparing and cardio a few times each month. I HATE it! Be that as it may, I likewise love it, in light of the fact that as troublesome all things considered at the time, it is justified, despite all the trouble all through the remainder of the day.puppy physical exercise

Also, I rest easy thinking about myself!

Your pooch can profit as well! I like to take my pooches for high force runs. I sit in a sidelong supine trike and let them pull for a few miles.

More often than not, as long as it is protected, I likewise enable them to establish the tone. Your pooch is a competitor and he needs the capacity to appreciate work out, REAL exercise! Exercise is additionally useful for his heart and body condition and joints.

Kindly help your canine out and furnish him with some genuine exercise every day! His body, his waistline, his circulatory strain and his mind needs it! The accompanying tips for beginning HIIT with your pooch are cordiality of SnootyPests.Com

Start Gently

In the event that you might want to begin HIIT with your canine, at that point it is imperative in the first place delicate sessions, especially if your pooch isn't accustomed to getting a great deal of activity. The most ideal approach to do this is to make the eruptions of force shorter, state 10 seconds, and the rest time frames longer, for instance 40 seconds. As you complete more HIIT sessions you will have the option to modify the proportions so that inevitably the extraordinary periods are longer and the rests are shorter.

Try not to Overdo It

Much the same as somebody who works out at a rec center, it is essential to let your pooch have rest days to recoup from the extreme exercise. Rest days are similarly as significant as exercise days as they let the muscles assemble and recuperate.

Keep it Short

The extraordinary thing about HIIT is that it doesn't require some investment to finish an exercise.

Keep the sessions short, around 10 minutes is sufficient, and make sure to heat up and chill off with some strolling or pull games first.

Make it Fun

You don't need to adhere to running and strolling for your HIIT session. Pick exercises your pooch will adore.

On the off chance that they love pursuing balls, at that point hurl a ball a lofty slope for them for a moment, at that point walk them for 30 seconds and rehash.

Get imaginative!

On the off chance that you might want to improve your own and your canine's wellness levels then high power interim preparing is an unquestionable requirement.

#2 Regular Physical Exercise

. . .

I can't state it enough, your canine isn't outside plotting his activity routine and intending to get fit. A walk around the square or a walk around a couple of miles isn't sufficient to tire your pooch. Once in a while I like to appreciate a few mile climb.

I likewise like urging my pooches to swim.

I locate that swimming will deplete my pooches decently fast, while strolling and climbing takes numerous long stretches of reliably thorough exercise; swimming is reasonably physically debilitating.

playing fetchMy hounds totally LOVE dock plunging.

You can likewise show your canine to pull loads, pull a truck, and pull a bike or yourself in inline skates (just as skijoring in the day off).

Draw coursing is additionally another fun physical game.

In any case, if strolling is all you're ready to do, don't be disheartened.

Fortunately satisfactory mental incitement is all you need so as to keep your canine's consideration on you!

You can make things energizing for him with these intellectually animating games to play while strolling him.

The Recall Game

．　．　．

Coming when called is likely THE MOST significant aptitude that you will ever show your canine. Be that as it may, individuals infrequently accept the open door to take a shot at this while they are on a stroll with their pooch on rope by them! Why not condition the pooch, regularly, that coming when called is a superb thing?

So while I am strolling, with my canine in heel position or even toward the finish of the chain (I don't permit any pulling) I start to run in reverse while calling my pooch to "come". I make it fun! I skip, I acclaim and I reward liberally in the event that he reacts rapidly and in a vivified manner.

In the event that I need to include more (and I generally do!) I get him to sit legitimately before me and afterward discover heel once more!

Push Ups

Ahhhhhh push-ups are one of my preferred activities to engage my pooch's brain and fumes his body!

These don't need to be done exactly at home in the middle of my four dividers! I love adding push-ups to a walk.puppy mental incitement

To begin with, let me clarify: when I state push-ups I am looking at having my pooch "sit", and afterward "down", and afterward "sit" in quick progression.

．　．　．

Furthermore, for an incredible video arrangement on the most proficient method to show these essential directions, click here.

To hone my pooch's listening abilities and acquiescence while I am strolling, I direction my canine to "down" (ideally while we are still moving) and afterward I request various "sits" and "downs" before at last remunerating him with a delectable treat or his preferred toy.

Stow away and Seek

Find the stowaway is another extraordinary game to play on a walk or at the recreation center, however you need two individuals! One individual should shoot away and locate a decent concealing spot, while the other individual occupies the pooch (or lets him watch first and foremost). At that point the concealing individual calls the pooch to "COME" all while commending him as he attempts to locate his proprietor.

"Fierceness, COME!!!! Great young lady, Good young lady, Good young lady, COME" You can't call once and afterward trust that he is persuaded to discover you. You should laud and spur him until he discovers you!

This is additionally a fun method to set that review or come order that we discussed before!

"COME" ought to be FUN! In the event that you reliably work both of the review games you will see your pooch's review boundlessly improve! Your pooch doesn't need to be a researcher to mess around while strolling.

Indeed, even the most youthful mutts and young doggies can profit by essentially changing your pace from moderate to quick or to slow. go running with your little dog

Changing pace keeps your canine animated and his emphasis on you! Circles are additionally fun!

Toss around to one side to keep your canine gazing toward you and to instruct him to escape your direction. Toss around to one side to propel him to stay aware of a quicker pace.

A great many people scarcely deal with acquiescence while they have their mutts out for a walk.

Their aim is just to go from guide A toward point B and back while they think they are giving their canine exercise. Be that as it may, strolling isn't the most ideal approach to practice your pooch. Furthermore, incidentally this is one reason hounds don't tune in to their proprietors while they are out of the house!

All together for your canine to hear you out while strolling, you should deal with preparing him while you are strolling. Disregard simply getting from direct A toward point B – chip away at rope preparing and mess around!

The #1 Way to Physically Exhaust Your Dog?

Put these things together for quick and complete depletion.

My most loved go-to when I need a drained pooch is getting them to perform dutifulness directions in a quick paced way and afterward I toss their ball to pursue as a prize.

For example, I get my hurl it and ball (I regularly utilize these in light of the fact that I can toss more remote) and my canine and request various directions; watch me, heel, sit, down, come back to heel, down moving and afterward I mark the finished arrangement of directions with a tick or a word and toss the ball the extent that I can for them to recover.

hounds love to fetchAs they quickly come back with the ball (or pull or whatever toy I am utilizing), I choose whether I will request them to drop the toy and afterward toss it once more, or in the event that I will request more compliance before I toss.

I blend it up!

I don't generally request similar practices in succession.

Furthermore, once in a while I will toss the ball or toy on numerous occasions before coming back to acquiescence. The pursuing the toy and recovering is extraordinary exercise for my pooches, physically. They are pursuing and quick and returning as quick as possible.

I additionally once in a while ricochet the ball hard, or hurl it so they can get it to give them assortment with their play. On the off chance that I take them out for HIIT I toss in certain alters of course, a few downs moving or sits moving and some heel. What's more, when my pooches are climbing or return from swimming I additionally request downs from a separation, or some fast eye to eye connection and center and behaving so I draw in their brain.

The best incitement comes when you connect all pieces of your canine!

The amount Exercise is Too Much for Your Puppy?

try not to utilize tennis balls in little dog preparing

Would you be able to practice your pup excessively? As per this article from the AKC, the appropriate response is in excess of a basic yes. "We might not have accurate estimations, however there are a couple of sound judgment contemplations that can assist you with thinking of an arrangement to keep your little dog dynamic and solid.

First off, think about your canine's breed. A Bulldog little dog and a Border Collie doggy will both love recess, yet a Border Collie will most likely have a higher exercise resistance than a Bulldog, also a higher warmth resilience for open air play.

Breed size issues, as well. There have been thinks about that show potential connections between an excessive amount of activity and orthopedic ailment in huge breed hounds. Driving your 8-week-old Great Dane for a two-mile walk each day, for example, is likely not a good thought, regardless of whether he could keep up. A great many people would not consider taking a littler breed pup for a climb that long, however with higher vitality levels, bigger breeds can trick us into deduction they need longer strolls than is beneficial for them.

Learning as much as you can about your breed is a decent spot to begin.

Huge and monster breeds develop rapidly and develop gradually, which may mean you need to put off specific exercises, such as hopping in readiness, until they are completely developed. doggy back-and-forth is useful for their teeth and gums

Toy breeds, then again, develop all the more rapidly yet require little, visit feedings for the duration of the day as doggies, which can mean you may need to change their activity in like manner.

All breeds require mental incitement, however high-drive, working breeds, for example, Belgian Malinois, Border Collies, and German Shepherd Dogs need more mental incitement than different breeds.

Fiery Dogs for Active People

No two mutts are actually similar, yet breed is a central point in deciding movement level. For example, many crowding and working canine breeds will in general be very dynamic. These high-vitality hounds need both mental and physical exercise to flourish. On the off chance that they don't have an outlet for their overabundance vitality, they may get ruinous or create different issues. Here are 10 of the most enthusiastic pooches that need a guardian who can stay aware of them.

Tip

Every day strolls alone probably won't be sufficient for some high-vitality hounds. Think about partaking in hound sports, for example, dexterity or flying circle, to give your canine extra mental and physical incitement.

Fun and Easy Ways to Exercise With Your Dog

Fringe Collie

fringe collie getting a frisbee on grass

Ivan/Getty Images

Fringe collies are incredibly keen, vigorous pooches. They are known for their common capacities in deftness and plate rivalries. They can make superb pets, on the whole and preeminent they need a vocation. Their common sense is to crowd, however they can channel that into pursuing toys or doing riddle games.

Breed Overview

Stature: 18 to 22 inches

WEIGHT: 30 to 55 pounds

PHYSICAL CHARACTERISTICS: Rough or smooth, medium-length coat; can be strong, bicolor, tricolor, merle, or sable; well-adjusted, athletic body

02

of 10

Australian Shepherd

two Australian shepherds holding a stay together

Rhonda Venezia Photographer/Getty Images

Australian shepherds likewise are profoundly shrewd and vivacious, exceeding expectations in hound sports. They were reared to group domesticated animals, so they will probably search out their own "work" through pursuing creatures or individuals. A few Aussies may act difficult or reserved if not given structure, preparing, and adequate exercise.

Breed Overview

Stature: 18 to 23 inches

. . .

WEIGHT: 40 to 65 pounds

PHYSICAL CHARACTERISTICS: Medium-length coat; well-adjusted body; hues incorporate dark, blue merle, red, and red merle

03

of 10

Australian Cattle Dog

Cows hound hopping

Joe Michl/Getty Images

Australian dairy cattle hounds are a dedicated, high-vitality breed. A canine that has the stamina to group dairy cattle throughout the day can without much of a stretch get exhausted as a pet except if it's given abundant exercise and mental incitement. Dairy cattle hounds exceed expectations all things considered pooch sports and will in general appreciate learning stunts and confuse games.

Breed Overview

Stature: 17 to 20 inches

. . .

WEIGHT: 30 to 50 pounds

PHYSICAL CHARACTERISTICS: Strong form; smooth twofold coat; hues incorporate blue and red with dark and tan markings

Jack Russell Terrier

Jack Russell terrier running in grass

@Hans Surfer/Getty Images

Numerous terrier breeds can be exceptionally lively, including Jack Russell terriers. These little canines surely aren't languid lap hounds. Without preparing and overwhelming day by day work out, they may channel their abundance vitality into burrowing, yapping, and other bothersome practices. Be that as it may, they regularly well in learning hound sports and different stunts.

Breed Overview

Tallness: 13 to 14 inches

. . .

WEIGHT: 13 to 17 pounds

PHYSICAL CHARACTERISTICS: Smooth or broken coat; hues incorporate white with dark, brown, or tan markings

Keep on 5 of 10 beneath.

05

of 10

Weimaraner

Running weimaraner

The Weimaraner was reared for chasing and keeps on having that drive to be moving, running long separations. These mutts will in general be cordial and warm, however some can be hyperactive. Without organized preparing and a colossal measure of activity every day, Weimaraners can get focused or ruinous.

Breed Overview

Stature: 23 to 27 inches

The Belgian Malinois regularly works for law implementation, and it needs some sort of employment to flourish. In the event that you pick a Malinois as a pet, let your pooch take an interest normally in hound sports. Notwithstanding adequate day by day physical exercise, nose work and following are incredible choices for mental incitement.

18 of the Easiest Dog Breeds to Train

Owning a canine accompanies a great deal of obligation. Pooches need a protected domain and a nutritious eating regimen. They need veterinary consideration. Furthermore, they need exercise, consideration, and a lot of preparing. It's no big surprise that notwithstanding scanning for a canine who's anything but difficult to possess, numerous individuals need a pooch who will effectively adapt new deceives (or figure out how to calm himself outside).

Honestly, despite everything you'll have to invest a lot of energy preparing your canine. What's more, hounds who are anything but difficult to prepare regularly still need loads of your time and vitality. Yet, the canines who are most effortless to prepare will rapidly connect directions with activities. What's more, more often than not, they'll need to satisfy you and adhere to your guidelines.

Look at the charming canine breeds that have a solid possibility of rapidly realizing what you instruct them.

1. Bernese mountain hound

Bernese mountain hound

Bernese mountain hound | iStock.com/RalphyS

The Bernese mountain hound is a well disposed breed that takes to preparing effectively. As per the AKC, this "delicate goliath" is mellow tempered and adores open air exercises. This breed needs a moderate degree of activity, which will as a rule prevent your canine from yelping or carrying on.

The Bernese Mountain Dog Club reports that "with the preparation basic for responsibility for huge working breed, Berners are commonly delicate, accommodating, and tolerant." But they do require a lot of association with individuals. Furthermore, the club prompts preparing should consistently utilize positive systems.

Next: A human satisfying canine who wants to joke around

2. Havanese

Havanese little dog running in grass with ball

Havanese | iStock.com/Dorottya_Mathe

The Havanese consistently needs to satisfy his proprietor. That implies he adores adapting new directions and stunts. Actually, the AKC reports the "Havanese are keen, trainable, and normal comedians." This pooch breed is a decent decision for fledgling canine proprietors.

Be that as it may, remember he needs organization and adores being the focal point of consideration. As indicated by the Havanese Club of America, the significant worry with a Havanese little dog "is to give satisfactory socialization to the puppy to turn into a productive member of society both in the home and the network. This normally includes introduction to a great deal of others and different mutts."

Next: A keen canine who needs to utilize his vitality satisfying his proprietor

3. Outskirt collie

Outskirt collie little dog

In case you're an accomplished pooch proprietor and just need a canine who will take to preparing admirably, you should think about an outskirt collie. The fringe collie has huge amounts of vitality yet needs to satisfy you. The AKC exhorts, "The uncanny knowledge, physicality, and trainability of outskirt collies have an ideal outlet in nimbleness work." Translation? This compulsive worker canine will never be a habitual slouch. So you'll have to use your very own portion vitality keeping him occupied.

The Border Collie Society of America reports you'll likewise need to set aside a few minutes for progressing preparing "in dutifulness, submission, compliance!" Activities, for example, dexterity, flyball, rally, crowding, and following, all empower your canine to adapt new mental abilities. Furthermore, they can assist you with giving your outskirt collie the incredible day by day practice he needs.

Next: A spunky little canine who's snappy to learn

4. Small schnauzer

Small schnauzer lying on the grass

Small schnauzer | iStock.com/Elen11

The small schnauzer thinks that its simple to adapt new directions. Be that as it may, you'll unquestionably to work to keep this high-vitality hound involved. Also, you'll need to prepare him not to bark too much. Luckily, the AKC clarifies, "This breed hungers for human friendship, which, joined with the breed's knowledge, makes him simple to prepare for a wide range of exercises. He is alert and spunky, yet in addition faithful to directions."

The American Miniature Schnauzer Club reports the breed profits by essential compliance preparing and continuous socialization. Be that as it may, they are "submissive and snappy to adapt, amazingly committed, fun loving, and exceptionally tender."

Next: A shockingly laid-back — and trainable — terrier

5. Fringe terrier

Two fringe terriers in the day off

The fringe terrier is frequently viewed as an exceptionally trainable pooch. What's more, he's laid-back for a terrier — however don't imagine that implies he won't require a great deal of movement. The AKC clarifies the outskirt terrier is "depicted as 'rock solid when working, however at home they're acceptable tempered, friendly, and trainable." With a lot of activity, they can live similarly as cheerfully in the city as in the nation.

As indicated by the Border Terrier Club of America, the outskirt terrier needs to satisfy you. "This makes it simple to prepare essential house habits, for example, housebreaking, strolling on a rope, disregarding trash, disregarding garments and children's toys, not hopping on individuals or furniture, sitting and staying, and coming when called (excepting the nearness of a squirrel or hare)."

Next: A peppy and perky mutts who take orders from you or your children

6. Fighter

fighter little dog

The fighter is an insightful and calm canine who adapts new directions effectively. As indicated by the AKC, these exceptionally dynamic pooches "appreciate physical and mental difficulties." But they are additionally "perky and fun loving. Their understanding and defensive nature have earned them a notoriety for being an incredible pooch for youngsters."

The American Boxer Club reports however numerous fighters prevail at execution occasions, the "same natural insight that makes him brisk to adapt likewise gives the fighter his very own brain." The club adds that a coach needs to remain "deliberate and quiet."
7. Doberman pinscher

. . .

Just experienced pooch proprietors ought to think about a Doberman pinscher. Be that as it may, in case you're ready to give predictable preparing and initiative, he can turn into an agreeable individual from your family. Simply recall Dobermans, in the same way as other different canines, can get ruinous and forceful in the event that you let them become constantly exhausted or forlorn.

As indicated by the AKC, the Doberman who is all around prepared and mingled "is a caring pet, a world-class family gatekeeper, [and] a flexible canine competitor." The Doberman Pinscher Club of America reports these pooches require canny taking care of yet are adaptable in exercises, including search and salvage, acquiescence, and work as a guide or treatment hound.

8. German shepherd

The German shepherd is anxious to please and prepared to work. What's more, as the AKC reports, this extremely dynamic breed needs standard mental and physical exercise. In any case, fans love the breed for its reliability, fearlessness, and "the capacity to learn and hold directions for a stunning number of particular occupations."

The German Shepherd Dog Club of America reports straightforward preparing should start the minute your doggy shows up home. A German shepherd doggy can get familiar with his name and essential directions as ahead of schedule as about two months old.

Next: A canine who's shrewd and bossy, however takes well to preparing

. . .

9. Pembroke Welsh corgi

The Pembroke Welsh corgi is a functioning little canine who cherishes having a vocation to do. The AKC clarifies, "The Pembroke reacts well to preparing and adores his family, however he may attempt to group you." Corgis (and corgi proprietors) advantage from acquiescence classes. What's more, the AKC guarantees, "The time you spend in preparing, particularly during the principal year of your pet's life, will be reimbursed many occasions over by giving you a polite buddy, one that is attached to you and your family for an amazing remainder."

The Pembroke Welsh Corgi Club of America that corgis "are astute canines, trainable and great with kids." Nonetheless, "this breed is splendid and bossy — in the event that you aren't in control, they will cheerfully accept the job and an issue is a lot harder to address than forestall."

10. Brilliant retriever

The brilliant retriever makes an incredible ally for beginner hound proprietors. This canine needs to please. What's more, as the AKC notes, "They have a blissful, fun loving way to deal with life and keep up this uncorrupt conduct for longer than some different breeds."

As indicated by the Golden Retriever Club of America, hounds — including brilliant retrievers — are issue solvers and learn by experimentation. Yet, your brilliant isn't the one in particular who will get the hang of during the way toward preparing. "As you show your canine the means important to get familiar with the acquiescence works out, he will react effectively or erroneously, and you should figure out how to react suitably," the club says.

Next: A fantastically famous breed that cherishes individuals and different pooches

11. Labrador retriever

three Labradors

Labrador retrievers | iStock.com/Lizcen

The Labrador retriever accepts the cake as the most famous pooch in the U.S. — and all things considered. The breed is anything but difficult to prepare, regardless of whether you need one as a family pooch or working canine. The AKC reports Labs mingle well with people and with different pooches. Be that as it may, you shouldn't "confound his laid-back character for low vitality. The Labrador retriever is very dynamic — he's never met a terrace he didn't care for." According to the Labrador Retriever Club, these canines are "anxious to please and non-forceful toward man or creature."

Next: A savvy and enthusiastic laborer that is anxious to please

12. Australian shepherd

Australian shepherd remaining in the grass

. . .

The Australian shepherd can get the hang of anything you can instruct him. Be that as it may, you have to keep him occupied and engaged. Actually, you'll presumably need to constantly devise new games and difficulties for this profoundly clever canine. As the American Kennel Club clarifies, this current breed's "solid work drive can make Aussies more pooch than an inactive pet proprietor may expect. Aussies are astoundingly astute, very equipped for outflanking a clueless beginner proprietor."

The United States Australian Shepherd Association reports these canines are exceptionally trainable and "effectively housebroken on the grounds that they are clever and anxious to please." But you'll have to channel your pooch's vitality to monitor his conduct.

Next: A terrier with an exceptionally cheerful demeanor

13. Norwich terrier

Norwich terrier on grass

The Norwich terrier is vigorous and needs a ton of action. Be that as it may, he's anything but difficult to prepare, and even amateur canine proprietors will have the option to deal with him. The AKC reports the Norwich terrier needs both physical and mental exercise. In any case, these pooches make "savvy, willing allies and can exceed expectations in an assortment of canine exercises."

The Norwich Terrier Club of America clarifies however the breed initially filled in as a working terrier, these mutts "were likewise esteemed for their amiable demeanor." Today, "the breed holds its unique chasing senses, little size, and joyful disposition so prized by early huntsmen on the two sides of the Atlantic."

Next: A pooch who gains from each and every experience

14. Papillon

The papillon is another canine who will effectively adapt new deceives however needs you to keep him involved. The AKC reports this "dynamic" hound breed likes exercise and takes to preparing. Their insight assumes a job in their trainability. However, furthermore, "it causes that they like to please and be with those they love."

The Papillon Club of America clarifies these canines are "cheerful, alarm, and inviting," however you should be a steady coach to draw out the best in your pooch. "Predictable, committed mentors thoroughly enjoy the inclination this breed has for pretty much anything. Yet, this is a breed that gains from each and every experience, and a conflicting mentor won't deliver steady outcomes — even with fundamental aptitudes like housebreaking."

Next: A social canine who doesn't care for being disregarded

. . .

15. Brussels griffon

brussels griffon hound outside

Brussels griffon hound | iStock.com/Onetouchspark

The Brussels griffon reliably positions as probably the most effortless canine to prepare. As the AKC notes, they are "social, amicable, and effectively prepared and will typically coexist well with other family pets and respectful youngsters." Just remember they're one of the more high-upkeep hound breeds since they want to remain nearby to their proprietors and don't care for being disregarded.

In any case, the American Brussels Griffon Association reports this breed "exceeds expectations in compliance (the show ring), submission, dexterity, rally preliminaries, following tests, and as treatment hounds."

Next: A breed that can adapt pretty much any assignment

16. Poodle

The standard poodle reliably positions as one of the most astute and respectful breeds — which can at times feel like a phenomenal mix. The AKC guarantees, "Poodles are insightful and effectively prepared to do various things. A portion of the exercises that poodles appreciate are following, chasing, nimbleness, and acquiescence."

. . .

The Poodle Club of America exhorts that "a poodle ought to be an individual from the family. Forthcoming proprietors of poodles ought to be prepared to give a fenced-in region in which the poodle can work out, or be set up to walk the poodle normally on a chain."

17. Rottweiler

The Rottweiler takes effectively to preparing, however he unquestionably needs work to keep him glad. As indicated by the AKC, this current pooch's "insight, perseverance and readiness to work make him reasonable as a police hound, herder, administration hound, treatment hound, compliance contender and dedicated friend." You'll have to prepare him on fundamental dutifulness directions, just as social aptitudes. What's more, you'll additionally need to outfit his regular regional senses. As the AKC puts it, "He needs to realize that you're in control, regardless of whether he is twice your size."

The American Rottweiler Club clarifies these mutts "need socialization, practice and animating mental difficulties. With these things, you will have a great partner; without them, your Rottweiler may get ruinous and crazy."

Next: A crowding master who needs to satisfy his proprietor

18. Shetland sheepdog

The Shetland sheepdog is a little yet extremely dynamic pooch that reliably performs well in deftness and other canine games — a demonstration of his capacity to learn. As per the AKC, you should take advantage of the breed's grouping legacy with "task-based exercise."

. . .

The American Shetland Sheepdog Association clarifies these canines "want to satisfy their proprietors and a colossal limit with regards to love and friendship." Additionally, "the Sheltie is uncommonly trainable and responsive, in addition to being a remarkable laborer in submission, grouping, and readiness preliminaries."

UNDERSTANDING MENTAL AND PHYSICAL EXERCISES FOR YOUR DOG AND BREED SELECTION

CHAPTER 4

I've generally been a functioning individual, so I concede I never felt I needed to work out. I didn't require a rec center; we live on a farm, and I joyfully handle my errands, which has constantly given me both a psychological and physical break from sitting in my home office.

While I'm outside breathing the natural air, I pull out the Chuckit and help our pooches get going as well. A functioning personality in a functioning body is the perfect, for pets and individuals both.

A couple of months back, however, I concluded that despite the fact that I was doing OK, I realized I could feel surprisingly better. Luckily for me, my better half, Teresa, is a specialist on diet and exercise, and she has since quite a while ago tried to do she says others should do. I accepted my significant other's recommendation (and my doctor's) and joined her for exercises in our home rec center. It was probably the best choice I've at any point made.

It's just plain obvious, I thought I had my wellness leveled out, yet I expected to investigate what I was doing and roll out certain improvements. The equivalent is frequently obvious with regards to your canine: No one type of activity fits each pooch, and, after its all said and done, what worked at one time may require changing from time to time.

Start With a Conversation With Your Veterinarian

Regardless of what age, size, shape, breed or blend of canine you have, you can't simply push him into an activity program until you realize he is solid. That has for some time been the guidance for individuals needing to improve their eating regimen and physical condition, and it bodes well for hounds. So observe your veterinarian before you start adding new exercises to your canine's day.

When your veterinarian gives you the approval, take a gander at your pooch, For certain mutts, the genuine multi-sport competitors in hide, practically any sort of activity is extraordinary and a greater amount of it is far and away superior. With different pooches, in any case, you have be cautious: Some sorts of activity are simply not reasonable for specific kinds of canines. Two sorts of canines specifically are probably going to be narrow minded of certain sorts of activity: Dogs with short faces, and pooches with short legs and long backs.

PUPPY NUTRITION AND HOUSE RULES, BASICS OF A GOOD ROUTINE

CHAPTER 5

Step by step instructions to Create House Rules For Your New Puppy

You're getting another little dog! This is an energizing time, and it's anything but difficult to fantasize pretty much all the fun things you'll do with a canine in your life. There's a ton you can do in readiness to ensure that your doggy's presentation into the family unit goes easily. It begins by making some house administers before your little dog even gets back home.

For what reason Do You Need Puppy House Rules?

Canines have their very own characteristic practices, not which will all be satisfactory in their new family unit, and a few practices could even be perilous, damaging, or unfortunate. By making a lot of house rules, you'll be telling your pup, directly from the earliest starting point, what is and isn't adequate.

This is all new for the little dog: he needs to change in accordance with his new family and new condition. On the off chance that everybody in the family is reliable with rules, it will assist him with realizing precisely what you expect of him, and what he can expect of you. The most ideal approach to do this is by making house rules for your doggy early.

beagle pup

How Do I Create House Rules?

All relatives ought to plunk down and make sense of the house manages together. Similarly as when you characterize desires for your children, consistency is vital, and if the entire family concedes to the standards, it's almost certain they'll adhere to them. At that point you'll have to conclude which are the most fundamental principles. Clearly a 20-page declaration of what your pooch can and can't do will be mistaking for everybody, including the pup. What's more, it'll make it a lot harder to remain reliable. Things being what they are, what's imperative to you?

imposing pup

A few Rules to Consider:

1. Where will you enable the pup to go in the house? A few people are OK with doggies having unfenced from the earliest starting point. Others build up specific regions of the house as no-hound zones, for example, the kitchen or an infant's room. You may need the doggy to remain on one story as it were. For some families, it's least demanding to hold the doggy to a little territory of the house during house-preparing.

2. Will you let the canine on the furnishings? Whatever you choose is OK for a modest, charming little dog may not be so incredible for a full-developed pooch. It's imperative to choose from the earliest starting point what the standard is. You can instruct him to remain off furniture totally, or you can prepare him to remain off the furniture

except if you give a particular order. Or then again, you may choose he's permitted to jump on one explicit household item, however not on others. Also, for certain individuals, furniture is an impeccably satisfactory spot for the canine to hang out. Whatever your inclination, make this standard before your little dog gets back home.

3. Who in the family is liable for what? It's simple enough before the little dog returns home for relatives to state they'll generally sustain the pooch or consistently take him out, however the fact of the matter is a significant distinctive issue. Choose now, before he turns out to be a piece of the family, what every individual's duty is.

4. Settle on a morning schedule. It tends to be hard enough planning calendars toward the beginning of the day, particularly in enormous families. Choose from the get-go when your little dog will go out and be bolstered.

5. The equivalent goes for a night schedule. Who bolsters him and when? Does he get a long, relaxed after-supper walk or a brisk excursion outside to put everything in order? Does he have a set sleep time or simply rest when he feels like it?

6. Where will the little dog rest? Will he be crated first floor, away from the rooms? Will he be crated in somebody's room? Will he rest on a canine bed in the corridor? Will he rest any place he needs? Indeed, even nestled up beside you in bed? Numerous proprietors decide to container the little dog around evening time, particularly until he's home prepared.

7. It is safe to say that you will enable your pooch to get treats from the supper table and get table pieces? Enabling your doggy to do this by any chance once can set up his desires, and he may stick around the table asking at each dinner. Beside the way that human nourishment may not be appropriate for hounds, this propensity can get irritating rapidly. Choose what the family rule is before the little dog returns home.

8. What directions will you use for fundamental acquiescence, as sit, remain, and come? Make a point to build up fundamental directions and additionally flags that everybody in the family unit will utilize reliably.

9. Would it be a good idea for you to let your little dog hop on

individuals? As adorable as a small pup is the point at which he welcomes you happily, is this a conduct you need to energize? As a rule, likely not. There's nothing charming about nearly getting dumbfounded by a 75-pound German Shepherd Dog. On the off chance that you need to show your canine not to hop, start as soon he gets back home.

When you've settled on the standards, post them in an obvious spot, as on the cooler, as a day by day suggestion to everybody of what their obligations are.

House Rules for Humans

young lady and doggy

House rules for your doggy aren't the main principles that should be set. Relatives, particularly kids, should likewise be sure about well-being and satisfactory conduct.

Kids must figure out how to deal with a little dog. As lovable as they seem to be, doggies aren't new extravagant toys or toys. Show the children not to pull the pooch's ears or tail or generally treat him like a lifeless thing.

Let the pup eat in harmony. Upsetting a pooch when he's eating can prompt tension and even nourishment hostility.

Try not to hit the pooch or shout at him. He doesn't comprehend what's he fouled up, it shows him nothing, and will cause trust issues.

Little dogs are common chewers and will most likely follow anything left on the floor; he doesn't have any acquaintance with it's your preferred shoe or new iPhone. For his security (and your very own mental soundness), get it and put it distant.

Carrying another little dog into the house is a genuine distinct advantage: the profundity of your affections for him and the delight he adds to your life may astound you. You can encourage a glad homecoming and a simpler change in the event that you make and adhere to some essential house rules from the earliest starting point. Your association with your canine will blossom with reasonable, steady rules.

UNDERSTANDING THE NEED OF YOURS PUPPY AND GUIDELINES

CHAPTER 6

N ourishing Your Puppy - The Complete Guide
All that you have to think about setting up your little dog with good dieting propensities to last them well into the adulthood.

Brilliant retriever little dog with bite toy in mouth

Nourishing your pup

Your little dog appears to be little now, yet they have a great deal of growing up to do in a short space of time! In only a year (as long as two years for bigger breeds) they'll become completely fledged grown-ups.

Meanwhile their bodies and minds need to grow unimaginably rapidly, and a lot of great pup nourishment causes them to arrive. They unquestionably need it, as a solid, vivacious little dog can consume up to twice the same number of calories as a grown-up hound!

Nourishing your little dog is likewise a significant piece of dealing with their wellbeing and joy. When they are mature enough to eat strong nourishment – typically when they are six to about two months old – it's a great opportunity to acquaint an eating regimen uniquely planned with address their issues.

What to sustain your little dog

Uncommonly defined doggy nourishments are the perfect eating routine for the most up to date individual from your family. This is on the grounds that they are finished and adjusted, which implies they contain everything your doggy needs to assist them with growing up soundly. There's no requirement for additional enhancements or bits of human nourishment – actually, these might accomplish more mischief than anything, regardless of how stubbornly they show you their pup hound eyes!

Here is the thing that to search for in the best little dog nourishment:

• High-calorie nourishment

Little dog nourishment is generally higher in calories than grown-up hound nourishment, as young doggies need a great deal of vitality for all the developing they need to do.

• Extra protein

Doggy nourishments will in general contain additional protein to help the sound improvement of their organs as they develop.

• Essential supplements

More significant levels of fundamental supplements like calcium, magnesium, iron, zinc and nutrient D are basic in the advancement of solid teeth and bones.

• Small kibble sizes

Made in littler kibble sizes to make it simpler to bite and swallow, pups frequently love crunching their evaporate nourishment, and will cheerfully eat their dinner across the board go.

The amount to sustain your doggy direct

The amount to nourish your little dog

All the time, a little dog will have eyes greater than their midsection! To get the equalization directly between what they need and overloading, give them modest quantities of doggy nourishment consistently. The right sum relies upon their age, size and any exhortation given to you by your vet. Take a stab at beginning with a tablespoon of nourishment around five times each day while your little dog is as yet sustaining from mum.

Here is a rule for the amount to encourage your doggy:

• From beginning to offer nourishment to weaning (normally two months) - 4-6 suppers per day

• From a few months - 4 suppers per day

• From four to a half year - 2-3 suppers per day

• Over a half year - 2 suppers per day (contingent upon breed)

Try not to be enticed to overload your little dog as an excess of could either agitated their belly or put pressure on their casing on the off chance that they put on a lot of weight in a brief timeframe. Neither of these are useful for your little dog's wellbeing, so take care when arranging their suppers.

Continuously read the encouraging directions on their doggy nourishment bundling cautiously – they should give you a decent beginning stage. The definite sum that you should encourage your pup can shift contingent upon their age, breed, any ailments and how enthusiastic they are – progressively fun loving pups will consume more vitality, so need more nourishment for fuel! Utilize our body condition apparatus to quantify your little dog and ensure that they're developing appropriately and aren't under or over weight.

Gauging your little dog consistently will assist you with making sure that they're the correct load for their age, size and breed. You can do this at home, or in case you're uncertain how, request that your vet show you or do it for you during a registration.

It's better for more youthful young doggies to eat pretty much nothing and regularly, as this won't overpower their creating processing – regardless of how eager they are tied in with completing their bowl of nourishment!

Pup nourishing and work out

Abstain from encouraging your little dog preceding or after exercise, and enable an hour to go among nourishing and action. It very well may be a smart thought to get your little dog into an early daily practice of having a rest straight after they eat to stay away from the danger of belly upsets or conceivably even an increasingly genuine condition, especially found in huge and mammoth breeds, where their stomach can grow and perhaps contort. This is called gastric swell (and torsion), and is a genuine ailment that requires dire veterinary consideration.

Pup sustaining and working out

Where to bolster your little dog

Here are a few rules for finding the ideal spot to bolster your little dog.

• Choose a calm spot

Ensure you feed the pup away from the buzzing about of a bustling house, where they can dive in, liberated from interferences.

• Choose a surface that can be effectively cleaned

Spot the nourishment on a tiled floor or a sustaining mat, and consistently serve the little dog nourishment in a perfect bowl.

• Keep youngsters from your doggy while they're eating

This will help maintain a strategic distance from them catapulting their nourishment or getting defensive over their dinner. On the off chance that you have different pooches in the house, feed them simultaneously, however separated, to abstain from battling and nourishment taking!

Instructions to bolster your little dog

Just as what to bolster a little dog, it's imperative to think about how to offer nourishment to them.

Wet pup nourishment is best served at room temperature, as it smells progressively appealing and is simpler to process. In the event that you store the nourishment in the ice chest, make sure to expel it an hour or so before supper times. It's fine to microwave wet nourishment for a brief span to warm it through, however ensure that it's just to room temperature and never hot.

Made in the USA
Middletown, DE
16 February 2020